THE DYNAMICS OF INFLATION

A Title from the Helen Kellogg Institute
for International Studies

THE DYNAMICS OF INFLATION

An Analysis of the Relations between Inflation, Public-sector Financial Fragility, Expectations, and Profit Margins

Antonio Kandir

UNIVERSITY OF NOTRE DAME PRESS
NOTRE DAME LONDON

Library of Congress Cataloging-in-Publication Data

Kandir, Antonio.
[Dinâmica da inflação. English]
The dynamics of inflation : an analysis of the relations between inflation, public-sector financial fragility, expectations, and profit margins / Antonio Kandir.
p. cm.
Translation of: A dinâmica da inflação.
Includes bibliographical references and index.
ISBN 0-268-00867-1
1. Inflation (Finance) I. Title.
HG229.K1813 1991
332.4'14—dc20 90-70859
CIP

Good theories are relevant abstractions,
and relevance alters as history moves on.
In economics, old theories are seldom wrong;
they have just become irrelevant.

Victoria Chick
Macro Economics After Keynes

CONTENTS

1

INTRODUCTION

The idea that in chronically inflationary economies inflation tends to have an inertial component has gained considerable ground in recent years.[1] This idea represents an important step forward in the understanding of inflationary processes in countries characterized by chronically high inflation rates. Nevertheless, we do not yet have an adequate analysis for understanding the acceleration of inflation in these countries. The prevailing diagnosis is the orthodox one, which says that the main factor in the acceleration is excessive demand. There are also the various schools of so-called heterodox or critical thinking which tend to highlight conflicts of distribution in a generic manner, without making any theoretical inroads into the issue of their dynamics.

The lack of an adequate diagnosis of the dynamics of the acceleration of inflation in such economies favors the implementation of anti-inflationary policies which, even when not strictly orthodox, tend to incorporate important elements from the conventional recipe book, albeit accompanied by heterodox treatment. These policies may induce stagnation for the countries in question, either because of their effects or because they are likely to recur, given that they do not attack the root causes of the acceleration.

One of the challenges facing anyone who sets out to analyze and propose stabilization policies is the fact that inflationary processes, like all economic processes, are not ahistorical.[2] As I shall try to show, inflation cannot be explained simply by affirming the existence of social actors who play differing roles in the economic process and who dispute a bigger share of the wealth to be distributed. Inflation is a more complex process than that, and can be understood only if a more structured, specific theory is developed. For the purposes of my argument, however, it is sufficient to recall that the problem of distribution is one of the various dimensions and determinants of the inflationary process. Thus when I assert that inflation is a historically determined phenomenon, my aim is to recall the simple fact that some of the basic factors underlying inflation change as history moves on. This is the case, for example, with changes in economic structures accompanying the expansion of capitalism: the emergence and actions of new social actors or changes in the social weight of the existing actors, changes in the relations between the state and the private sector, changes in the division of labor and in the organization and distribution of financial flows at the international level, among others, permanently revolutionize some of the determinants of inflationary processes.

In the specific case of economies undergoing adjustment[3]—and on which this study focuses attention—a new historical stage is begun by such adjustment processes as far as the dynamics of inflation is concerned. They radically transform the basis for capitalist circulation by introducing new elements into the dynamics of inflation, making these economies vulnerable to the acceleration of inflation even in the absence of conventional shocks, such as shortages of agricultural products or changes in the exchange rate. This endogenization of shocks, caused by the adjustment process, considerably complicates the task of designing stabilization policies, and in general the latter difficulty is insufficiently taken into account.

In view of the above remarks, let me sum up by saying that this book was written with two main aims in mind. The first was to develop a theoretical proposition for the study of the acceleration of inflation in the context determined by the adjustment processes which chronically inflationary economies with significantly complex productive structures encounter.[4] The second aim was to demonstrate that because of adjustment these economies tend to move toward a situation where inflation begins to present an endogenous acceleration component which, once it has been incorporated into the dynamics of inflation, may raise serious problems for all kinds of stabilization policy.

How will I attempt to develop my arguments? More generally, what is the most suitable form of argument for discussing the question of inflation? It is important to stress right away that empiricism will not take us very far, especially in this terrain. This is because capitalism relies on relations of interdependence between the public and the private, the real and the financial worlds, and between economic sectors and social classes which lead to different levels of correlation between the economic variables relevant to the study of inflationary processes:

> High fiscal deficits, inconsistencies in pricing, and resistance to reductions in the pace at which prices and wages rise usually occur together and act reciprocally on one another: once inflation has gotten moving it seems hard to identify a clearcut cause.[5] A similar phenomenon arises when we consider price variations from one period to another. It is often observed that at certain moments the amount of money increases faster than prices; at others wages, or the exchange rate, or some other group of prices surge ahead; at other moments again, prices rise without any apparent reason becoming clear. These sporadic advances and retreats do not define the 'type' of inflation at any moment, but rather reflect the erratic nature of pricing. (Heymann 1986)

These remarks are not intended to deny the usefulness of a statistical approach to the study of inflation. Without doubt statistical tools are important to an analysis of the problem. But their use should be secondary in that they should be preceded by an exposition that clearly brings out the theoretical framework appropriate to the development of statistical and simulation exercises. For these reasons, I first put forward a theoretical discussion of the problem, which must be prior to any analysis of concrete situations.

The first difficulty arising in an approach of this kind is the existence of an enormous variety of theoretical alternatives, very often based on only vaguely differentiated arguments. This variety partly derives from simple problems of construction and academic debate. Nevertheless, insuperable differences of opinion do exist, as a result of the ideologically determined atmosphere in which economic thought is enveloped.

On this subject, Dow presents three explanations for the permanent discord among schools of economists and lends support to the interpretation of Myrdal (1953) who, in Dow's own summary, asserts the following:

> It is in the nature of economics that there will be disagreements; while these may have ideological elements, ideology cannot be eradicated from theory. If this is the case, denial of the existence of valid disagreements should be regarded with some suspicion. (Dow 1985, 1)

In an ideologically heterogeneous society, there is a process of theoretical differentiation which, unless it is clearly acknowledged and respected, tends to transform the discussion of specific economic issues into a virtual exercise in "collective torture" and/or "rhetorical muscle-flexing."[6]

Therefore, although I am no admirer of such exercises, it is important to start by establishing a criterion for classifying theories of inflation. This criterion will permit me to express more clearly my disagreement with some theories and define the theoretical perspective on which this book is based. Chapter 2 addresses this problem and classifies theories of inflation in accordance with their microfoundations.

Chapter 3 contains a critical analysis of the most influential theories of inflation,[7] with the particular aim of characterizing them according to their microfoundations as per the scheme proposed in chapter 2. I try to demonstrate the inadequacy of existing theories of inflation, especially in view of the lack of integration between the macroeconomic and microeconomic levels. Such integration is needed to understand the dynamics of prices under conditions of high instability.

Building on the arguments presented in chapters 2 and 3, chapter 4 takes the first step towards developing a theoretical analysis that accounts for contemporary inflation in the countries in question,[8] i.e., developing an overall framework appropriate for the study of the short-run dynamics of desired markups.

The basic idea starts from recent critiques by post-Keynesian economists centering on the theoretical inadequacy of studying contemporary inflation by means of analytical models which use the notion of normal prices as a representation of the pricing process. According to such models, any acceleration of inflation results from a variation in costs (imported raw materials and wages). The basic critique is that under conditions of high instability the desired markups may vary conjuncturally to a significant extent, and thus begin to play an active role in determining changes in the inflation rate.

In sharing the fundamental points of this critique, I start from the contention that while under certain circumstances wages may accelerate inflation, they tend to play a very short-lived role as dynamic agents of sustained acceleration of inflation. This starting-point derives from the observation that both accelerated inflation in itself and the economic policies normally implemented in such situations tend to discourage investment, leading to a slowdown in economic activity and hence, ultimately, to a stabilization of real wages. Thus in order to understand how the acceleration is sustained, it is necessary to examine other causes of variation in the inflation rate. More specifically, in the context of high instability characteristic of present-day capitalism, desired markups play a fundamental role in producing such variations. So in order to understand the dynamics of acceleration it is necessary to comprehend the determinants of short-run variations in desired markups in every specific historical situation.

The first elementary question requiring an answer, then, is what role is played by prices under contemporary capitalism. There are grounds for questioning the basic idea in conventional thinking, which is that prices result from a process of collective arbitration of the distribution of a given production, in which the crucial dynamic element is the mutability of individual consumers' desires as they exercise their freedom of choice. As I point out in chapter 4, prices are the result of a complex process of decision making by oligopolies, driven by the search to maximize their power to appropriate wealth as it expands. Although the market does tell them about the outcome of their decisions, firms use this information, among other things, to set new prices as only one part of a simultaneous arbitration of prices, investment, and financing in accordance with their changing strategies. This, in turn, determines the trajectory of inflation, since in the medium-term wages are passive.

In short, chapter 4 discusses from a post-Keynesian perspective the factors determining conjunctural variation in desired markups. It begins with the elementary question of the nature of prices in a capitalist economy, moving on to identify their main dimensions and rules of motion. The final aim is to arrive at an analytical synthesis capable of explaining the interactions between the various elements which influence their dynamics.

Having established a theoretical framework in which to analyze conjunctural variations in desired markups and recognized the historical nature of inflationary processes, in chapter 5 I further specify the general formula set forth in chapter 4 so as to apply it to understand variations in desired markups in economies with significantly complex structures, chronic inflation, and adjustment processes under way. To this end some preliminary remarks are made on the nature of adjustment processes and their effects on the variables which are critical to the pricing process, particularly the financial fragility of the public sector.[9] The idea is to show that expectations about the future prices of public-fiscal goods[10] and exchange goods[11] assume importance in determining desired markups.

The point I shall endeavor to prove through these arguments is that attempts at adjustment lead to pressures for changes in relative prices between sectors with different patterns of use of these goods; and that this in turn leads to an acceleration of inflation that is sustained for as long as the adjustment is considered incomplete.

Chapter 6 deals with the nature of the acceleration and its various components. A model is used to show the universe of interactions among specific economic processes which may lead to endogenization of this acceleration in economies of the type in question. In other words, under certain circumstances the acceleration tends to be sustained by the interaction of several processes, among which the most important are the financial fragility of the public sector, the rise in the user cost of public-fiscal goods, and the pressure for differentiation in desired markups, this latter being a function of each particular productive structure.

To demonstrate these points I first develop a simple model of inflation, designed solely to highlight the role of what I term the user-cost index of public-fiscal goods in the dynamics of inflation. I then discuss the basic determinants of this index and analyze its dynamic components. The next step is to propose a model which attempts to account for the interactions between the user-cost index of public-fiscal goods, the inflation acceleration rate, and the financial fragility of the public sector.

With the aid of the models developed in chapter 6, it is possible to show the limits and problems of the stabilization policies that have been implemented to reduce inflation or contain its acceleration when there is an endogenous component of acceleration with the characteristics outlined above.

The last chapter presents some brief remarks underlining the key aspects of the arguments developed in the main sections.

2

A CLASSIFICATION OF THEORIES OF INFLATION

Inflation manifests itself as a macroeconomic problem, that is, a sustained rise in the general level of prices. For the various schools of quantity theory of money, inflation has always been a problem which can be explained theoretically at the strictly macroeconomic level. With a greater or lesser degree of sophistication, these schools believe that relative prices are formed in the real sphere, while the general price level results from the interaction between movements of macroeconomic variables, among which the pace of monetary expansion has decisive importance.[1]

However, the sphere which must be theoretically analyzed to obtain an understanding of the dynamics of inflation cannot be derived automatically from the form in which inflation manifests itself. On the contrary, an understanding of inflation presupposes a theoretical grasp of the pricing process, given that the general price level is merely an abstract entity which aggregates all the various prices at this level. That is not to claim that a microeconomic approach would be sufficient for the theoretical analysis of inflation: nothing could be further from the approach I consider necessary. To affirm the opposite would be to assume that macroeconomic phenomena do not interfere in the dynamics of inflation. As I show in chapters 4, 5, and 6, a theoretical understanding of the inflationary process requires integrating the microeconomic and macroeconomic levels of analysis. The point to be stressed here is the impossibility of developing such an understanding without a theoretical insight into the pricing process. In chapters 3 and 4, I show that economic theory has not yet developed an analysis of pricing appropriate to an understanding of the inflation process under conditions of great instability.

For these reasons, a classification of theories of inflation according to their microfoundations will be useful as a basis for the further elaboration of my argument, both in regard to a critique of existing theories and as an introduction to my own conception of the inflationary process in countries with a significantly complex productive structure, chronic inflation, and adjustment process under way.

2.1 The Microfoundations of Theories of Inflation

It must be stressed that a classification of theories of inflation according to their microfoundations is not a way of characterizing them completely, nor does it eliminate the need to discuss them in their totality. There is no simple one-to-one correspondence between theories and classes of theory. A particular classification may contain more than one theory. However, when dealing with the problem of inflation, this type of classification facilitates theoretical discussion by making explicit the basic structure of determination of price variations in each theory, as this is a crucial aspect of the way in which a theory analyzes the dynamics of inflation.

The microfoundations of theories of inflation can be characterized in view of the two dimensions of determination of price variation—the locus of definition of price variation and the presumed pattern of formation of expectations—and the conception of the economic structure assumed by the theory.[2] Throughout the evolution of economic thought, two main alternative types of determination of price variation have been established: the Walrasian and the Marshall-Kaleckian.[3]

The Walrasian type. In a Walrasian economy, the existence of a fictitious auctioneer guarantees the adjustment of markets where demand and supply are in disequilibrium. The basic principle of adjustment is as follows: Transactions are not performed as long as there is excess demand or supply. For a reversible period of time, the "auctioneer" creates the conditions for price variation (for in this type of economy economic agents only decide quantities) until the excess demand or supply disappears. Thus the concept of equilibrium implicit in the Walrasian view attributes to prices the fundamental role of adjusters of the system, which they perform by varying. Their variations are understood as immediate expressions of market imbalances which could be understood in a more general sense as both current and prospective disequilibria.[4]

The Marshall-Kaleckian type. In this case the locus of price determination is the firm. Rather than directly expressing the subjective preferences of the various economic agents or merely being adjustment variables in a system of general equilibrium, prices function directly as a guarantee of the desired profit rate for a firm dealing with an objective cost structure. Although they cannot be entirely explained by the logic of individual capital accumulation, prices are fundamentally determined by this logic.

As to the patterns of expectation formation which qualify the above types, contemporary theories involve three basic formulations: adaptive expectations, rational expectations, and conditioned expectations. A detailed discussion of these formulations will be left for later, since it will be more appropriate to characterize and differentiate them as the various theories are themselves being discussed. For the time being a brief introduction to each one will suffice.

Adaptive expectations. This approach assumes that expectations are formed in such a way that they can be represented as a simple function of past expectations, with the addition of a term for correction corresponding to a fraction of the errors committed in the past.

Rational expectations. This approach assumes that expectations are formed as follows: The economic agents seek out all the available information, with the search for information going as far as the point at which the marginal cost of obtaining and processing it equals the marginal benefit obtained from such a search. Based on such information, expectations are formed just as foreseen by the models through which the agents understand the economy.[5] Economic agents do not commit systematic errors; expectations are formed in such a way that they are normally distributed around the correct prediction; expectations may change radically, regardless of their behavior in the past.[6]

Conditioned expectations. This approach assumes that although the economic agents may use all available information in the best manner possible, changes in expectations are conditioned by the fact that the agents know that all economic agents take decisions under conditions of uncertainty. As Keynes pointed out, in this context agents try to obtain guidance from conventions which in many cases have as their reference point the evolution of variables in the past.[7] Far from reflecting irrational behavior, this way of modeling expectations acknowledges the rationality of economic agents—who, under conditions of uncertainty, attempt to follow conventions and conclude contracts—as well as the implications of the asynchronous nature of the many contracts existing in an economy.[8]

Finally, as regards the structure of capitalist economies, theories of inflation can be classed in accordance with two antagonistic conceptions, i.e., whether a capitalist economy is seen as an inherently stable structure or as an inherently unstable one. The former conception recognizes the existence of so high a degree of interdependence between economic agents that their plans and/or actions establish counterweights to the plans and actions of other agents, which tends to lead them to situations where their individual plans are made compatible. The period of time required for the effects of these counterweights to come into force varies with the school of mainstream macroeconomics one takes.[9] The basic idea is that there are forces which tend to balance out the various individual plans, and the different schools diverge only as to the number and quality of the restrictions to which analytical models are subject. In short, all the schools in question conceive the capitalist system as a stable system in the sense that they recognize that there are stabilizing mechanisms in operation and that they can at most be dampened or attenuated. Moreover, they all reduce expectations to a passive phenomenon, whose only role is to assist in establishing a given pattern of adjustment between one equilibrium and another.

The second conception (which sees a capitalist economy as being an inherently unstable structure) is built on the recognition that economic agents have to deal with radical uncertainty. This uncertainty, which should not be confused with a mere calculation or risks, as Keynes warned, derives from the fact that economic agents have decision-making autonomy and that time is irreversible. The irreversibility of time (in contrast with the various schools of mainstream macroeconomics, all of which take time as being reversible) means that the isolated decisions made by the various economic agents agents are crucially important, because once implemented they have consequences which cannot be fully reversed without costs. This irreversibility is especially serious when investment decisions are considered, given that these entail the commitment of fixed assets, which have little or no liquidity.[10] As Possas has underlined (1986), however far investors use conventional behavior as a guide, expectations are grounded in what Keynes calls a fragile "state of confidence", which is inversely proportional to the certainty present in the expectations formulated. Since they are made in such precarious situations and represent such a heavy responsibility for those who make them—in view of their importance and their irreversible nature—investment decisions hence become the elements that define a capitalist economic structure as unstable.[11]

Thus theories of inflation can be classified according to the various possible combinations[12] of the two basic types of price determination with the three models for formation of expectations and the two conceptions of the structure of the capitalist system. Each combination represents one type of microfoundation for theories of inflation (see table 1 on the following page).

In the next chapter I discuss monetarist, new classical, and neostructuralist theories of inflation, attempting wherever possible to highlight their microfoundations.

Table 1

Classification of Theories of Inflation
According To Their Microfoundations

<table>
<tr><th rowspan="4">Formation of expectations</th><th colspan="3">Price determination type</th></tr>
<tr><th colspan="3">Marshall-Kaleckian</th></tr>
<tr><th rowspan="2">Walrasian</th><th colspan="2">Conception of economic structure</th></tr>
<tr><th>Stable</th><th>Unstable</th></tr>
<tr><td>Adaptive expectations</td><td>Monetarist</td><td></td><td></td></tr>
<tr><td>Rational expectations</td><td>New classical</td><td></td><td></td></tr>
<tr><td>Conditioned expectations</td><td></td><td>Neo-structuralist</td><td>Post-Keynesian</td></tr>
</table>

3

A CRITICAL EXAMINATION OF THE MONETARIST, NEW CLASSICAL, AND NEOSTRUCTURALIST APPROACHES

3.1 A Walrasian Theory with Adaptive Expectations: Monetarism

Among the various interpretations of the inflationary process based on the Walrasian model of price variation is the monetarist analysis, which sees inflation as being essentially a monetary process: "Inflation is everywhere and anywhere a monetary phenomenon" (Friedman 1968).

3.1.1 *Preliminary Comments*

Before presenting the basic aspects of monetarism and discussing the reasons for its widespread influence, preliminary comments are in order. First, monetarism is not just a specific analysis of the inflationary process. It is a theoretical endeavor elaborated in opposition to the type of macroeconomic thought which predominated up to the end of the 1960s,[1] especially regarding what might be called the activist view of economic policy.[2] Secondly, it must be stressed that the main arguments of the monetarists have become deeply engraved in the minds of most economists, so that many of those who do not call themselves monetarists nonetheless make ample use of their concepts.

Partly for the above reasons, monetarist thought can be characterized in a number of different ways. According to one of its main exponents, Laidler, there have been several recent attempts to specify the fundamental characteristics of monetarism, particularly in the works of James Boughton (1977), Karl Brunner (1970), Victoria Chick (1973), David Cobham (1978), Timothy Congden (1978), Harry Johnson (1972),

Nicholas Kaldor (1970), Franco Modigliani (1977), Thomas Mayer (1978), and Douglas Purvis (1980). In addition there are the writings of Laidler himself (1981) and of Helmut Frisch (1983). In line with the latter's argument, we can say that an analysis is monetarist when it explicitly or implicitly assumes the following four propositions:

> (a) the private sector of an economy is inherently stable; the economic system returns automatically to full-employment equilibrium after a disturbance; the unemployment rate resumes its natural level;
> (b) any rate of growth in the money supply is compatible with a full-employment equilibrium, despite differing outcomes as regards the inflation rate;
> (c) a change in the rate of growth of the money supply initially alters the rate of real growth of the economy (and hence the unemployment rate); in the long run this real effect disappears and only a permanent rise in the inflation rate remains (acceleration theorem);
> (d) there is rejection of any economic policy of demand activism, whether fiscal or monetary, and preference for long-term monetary policies established through rules or targets." (Frisch 1983, 91–92).

3.1.2 *The Monetarist Attack*

Before presenting the monetarists' analysis of inflation, it is worth recalling that the impact of their arguments was mainly due to the failure of the neoclassical analysis to explain the phenomenon of stagflation. The conventional understanding of inflation was based until the late 1960s on a statistical formulation by Phillips (1958), later developed theoretically by Lipsey (1960) into a concept which stated that unemployment and inflation are opposite poles.[3] In other words, through its economic policies society can find a way out of one of these two problems provided it accepts the other. It is a question of making a political choice, the argument ran, and once policy makers have been correctly informed of this, the appropriate administration of monetary and fiscal instruments will do the rest.

In view of the perplexity of the so-called Keynesians over this new phenomena of contemporary capitalism, Milton

Friedman formulated an explanation for stagflation, based on his monetary theory of nominal income (1956), on Cagan's model of expectation formation (1956), and on his own interpretation of the Phillips curve.

In order to propose an alternative analysis of inflation, Friedman had to provide a convincing explanation for the fact that Keynesian policies aimed at an expansion of effective demand really made the level of employment rise. How could an alternative explanation for this Keynesian determination of employment expansion be found? How could he explain the possibility that employment was elastic without resorting to the neoclassical idea that the labor market conditions determined employment? To address these issues, Friedman introduced expectations as a factor in determining neoclassical equilibrium in the labor market.

Friedman's argument can be seen as a radical alteration to the relations between markets in goods and labor as proposed by Lipsey (1960).[4] In the neoclassical analysis, it had been understood hitherto that monetary and fiscal policies would be combined so as to create an equilibrium in the goods market, which in turn would produce a demand for labor, and the latter when faced with supply would determine nominal wages.[5]

Friedman (1968) inverted the argument by internalizing expectations in the analytical structure of the labor market and by reinstating analysis of that market through the concept of real wages, albeit modified to read "expected real wages".[6] He endeavored to show that the reduction in the level of employment resulting from an active economic policy is caused not by increases in effective demand but by the fact that for a period workers underestimate price rises.[7] The essential condition for employment to expand according to the neoclassical paradigm is a drop in real wages, since this is the only way for a firm seeking to maximize profits to demand more labor if its marginal productivity is constant. As Friedman explained it, this necessary cut in real wages would occur through the erroneous forecast made by wage earners about price evolution. The gap between expected real wages and actual real wages, once perceived by the employer, would be the basis for a rise in employment. Figure 1 shows this movement: DLB is the labor demand curve, which has a diminishing relation to real wages (w/p); SLB is the labor supply curve, which increases as a function of real wages. The level of employment L_e is given by the point at which the two curves intersect, also the point which establishes the equilibrium real wage $(w/p)^0$. This equilibrium occurs when workers correctly forecast prices $p = p'$, where p' is the forecast rate of variation in prices of goods consumed by workers. If $p > p'$, i.e., if workers underestimate the rate of price variation, the curve SLB shifts vertically downward by a distance corresponding to the underestimation of price variation $p - p'$, causing an expansion of employment equivalent to $L_1 - L_0$.

However, according to Friedman, sooner or later the wage-earners realize their mistake. Once the actual variation of prices resulting from monetary expansion, and hence the correct amount of prospective real wages, is perceived, there should be a drop in the labor supply with the restoration of that portion of the unemployment level which had been artificially removed (so Friedman argues) by a mere temporary illusion about price evolution. In graphic terms, there would be a vertical rise in the curve SLB corresponding to the adjustment in workers' forecasts. The trade-off represented by the Phillips curve between wage variation and unemployment would prevail only in the short run. Thus from the analytical standpoint an expansionist policy would be translated into movements along a conventional Phillips curve only in the short run. In the long run the Phillips curve itself would shift, and would in fact be vertical.

This analysis arrives at what is known as the accelerationist version of the Phillips curve,[8] where in the short run the choice has to be made between unemployment and inflation at higher rates than expected, or else between unemployment today and unemployment tomorrow.[9] In analytical terms this version is arrived at through the expressions for labor demand and supply developed by the neoclassical school. Simonsen (1983) shows that labor demand in the neoclassical formulation can be represented by the expression:

$$w - p = a + \log b - (1 - b)n \qquad (1)$$

where:

- a and b are the parameters of a log-linear aggregate production function:
- w is the Naperian logarithm of money wages;
- p is the Naperian logarithm of prices;
- n is the Naperian logarithm of employment.

On the other hand, labor supply can be represented by a log-linear relationship of the following type:

$$n_s = d + e(w - p) \tag{2}$$

where:

- n_s is the Naperian logarithm of labor supply;
- d and e are parameters of the log-linear curve of labor supply.

Based on these expressions and on the assumptions of Friedman's analysis, Simonsen arrives at the following expression for the Phillips curve in Figure 1.

$$y - y_p = k \cdot (z - z') \tag{3}$$

where:

- y is the Naperian logarithm of the product;
- y_p is the Naperian logarithm of the potential product;
- z is inflation;
- z' is expected inflation;
- k is a parameter.

If we change the expression slightly, we can see that the accelerationist version of the Phillips curve establishes that:

$$z = z' + 1/k(y - y_p) \tag{4}$$

which is equivalent to saying that inflation is the result of two components, one of which is expectations (z') and the other acceleration ($1/k(y-y_p)$), corresponding to increases in the expected inflation rate in proportion to the differences between the actual product and the product corresponding to the natural unemployment rate, the latter situations being caused by activist economic policy.

Figure 1

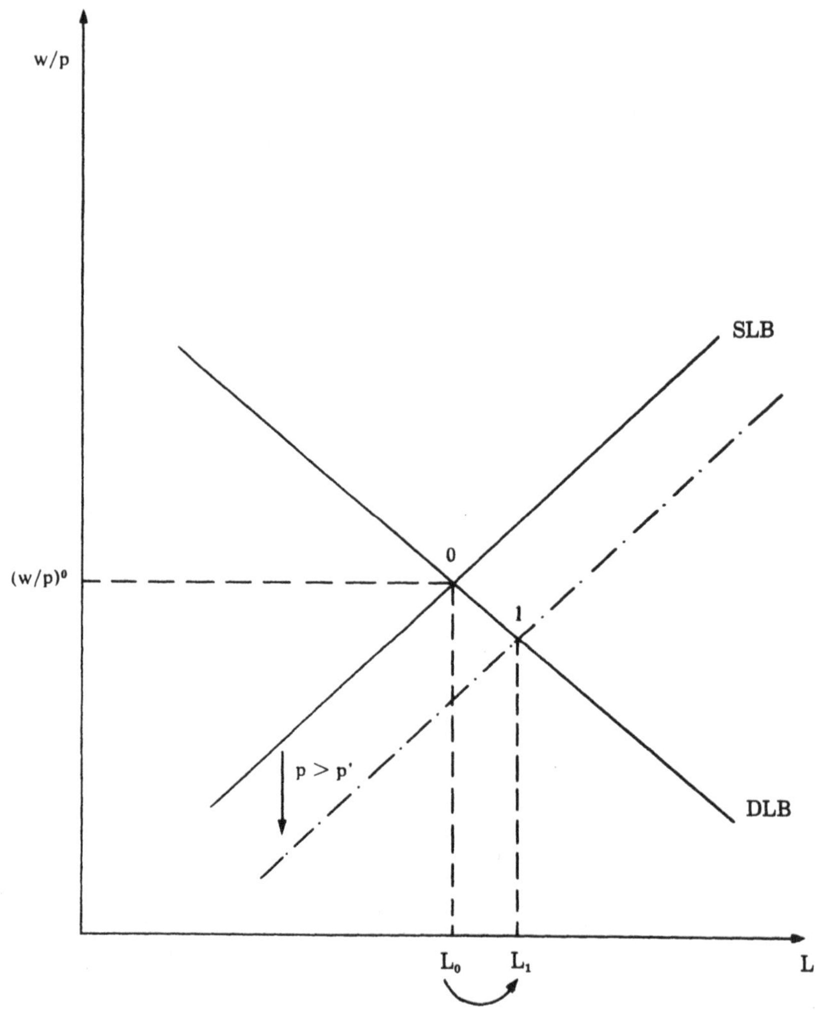

A key point in Friedman's analysis is the differing perception of price variation among workers and employers. As mentioned above, it is essential to Friedman's argument that wage-earners are slow to perceive price increases. The basic idea is that economic agents form their expectations in an adaptive manner. This idea was first put forward by Cagan

(1956), who modeled the expectation formation process under the assumption that economic agents correct their expectations by a process in which a fraction of the mistake made is added to the previous prediction.

One point in the argument is not clear, however. Why should the wage-earners be slower to perceive price variation? Some analysts claim that this point is confused in Friedman's argument. According to Swaelen, Friedman would reply "by saying that the former (the employers) are the ones who see prices on the goods market rise as demand for their products rises. But if the workers are the ones who demand these goods they should perceive the rise in prices at the same time! An unresolved question" (Swaelen 1982, 62).

Nevertheless, there are reasonable explanations for the phenomenon, based on the idea that employers and employees are interested in different kinds of information and that the former have in actual fact higher quality information which is simpler and more accessible:

> The assumption of money illusion is regarded by rational expectations theorists as irrational, constituting an ad hoc adjustment to macro models, insufficiently backed up with microfoundations. But slow responses can still be justified on the grounds of imperfect information (see Laidler, 1981). Employers, for example, have control over, as well as current information on, their product prices; these are the prices relevant to their price level expectations for the purposes of calculating the real wage. Workers on the other hand are interested in the general price level over which they have no control and only partial information ex post. (Dow 1985, 146)[10]

3.1.3 *The monetarist model*

From what has been expounded so far, it is possible to understand no more than the basis for an analysis of the inflationary process in accordance with the monetarist version. The monetarists' analysis proper depends on further theoretical elements. What is a monetary impulse? What are its effects? How do the adjustments between short-term and long-term situations take place in monetarist analysis?

To answer these questions I present the monetarist model in its most up-to-date version, as summed up in the argument of Frisch (1983) based on the work of J. Vanderkamp (1975). According to this argument, a standard model of monetarist ideas about the inflationary process can be represented by three basic equations, set out below and illustrated schematically in figures 2 and 3:

$$m_t = x_t + \pi_t \tag{5}$$

curve FF: quantitative equation;

$$\pi_t = \pi_t{}^* - b \cdot (\mu_t - \mu^*) \tag{6}$$

curve R: linearized version of Phillips curve with hypothesis of a natural rate of unemployment;

$$\mu_t - \mu_{t-1} = -a \cdot (x_t - x_t{}^*) \tag{7}$$

curve OK: Okun's law;
where:

m_t is the rate of growth in the money supply;
x_t is the rate of real growth in income;
$x_t{}^*$ is the anticipated trend rate of real income growth;
π_t is the inflation rate;
$\pi_t{}^*$ is the expected inflation rate;
μ_t is the level of unemployment;
μ^* is the natural rate of unemployment;
a and b are parameters.

According to the monetarist argument, when a positive monetary impulse occurs—i.e., when there is monetary expansion in excess of the sum total of expected inflation and the expected rate of real growth in income throughout the economy—there tends to be real growth which is unexpected in the short term, accompanied by an acceleration of the inflation rate.[11] Just how the monetary impulse is spread over increases in the rates of real growth and increases in the inflation rate is not important for the purposes of this argument. What matters is that when the rate of growth of the product accelerates, the level of unemployment drops below its natural level, which according to Friedman corresponds to frictional unemployment. The overemployment brought about by unexpected growth in the stock of money signals an imbalance between demand and supply, which translates into an acceleration of the inflation rate, via the Phillips curve in its Friedmanian version.[12] The rise in the inflation rate, given that the rate of monetary expansion remains constant, tends to cause a slowdown in the economic growth rate[13] and in the growth rate of overemployment, since the accelerating inflation leads to higher demand for money. Nonetheless, because of overemployment the inflation rate continues to rise while the growth rate declines until it returns to its initial value and the inflation rate shows an increment of equal magnitude to the initial unexpected increase in the rate of monetary expansion. This process is synthesized in figures 2 and 3. The amount the rate of monetary expansion rises beyond the expected rate corresponds to a leftward shift in curve FF; as a result, the inflation rate, which was zero and associated with point $x = x^*$ (real growth rate equal to the expected growth rate), becomes π_a, associated with a growth rate x_a higher than the expected growth rate x^*. The sum of the increments in the inflation rate and real growth rate is equal to the vertical shift in the curve FF. However, when unemployment is pushed beyond its natural level, growth $x_a > x^*$ moves leftward the curve representing Okun's law, which is in the lower right-hand quadrant of the figures. The shift continues until the rate of growth of real product returns to its initial position x^* and the inflation rate is raised to a value equal to the vertical shift in curve FF.

In short, the basic idea is that any unexpected increase in money supply, expressed by the inequality $m_t > x_t^* + \pi_t^*$, tends to trigger a process of acceleration caused by real growth of the product in excess of the expected rate. This variation in product growth rates alters the basic parameters of Okun's law because of the reduction in unemployment, and this alteration tends to lead to a convergence between the rise in inflation and the drop in the rate of real economic growth. The process ends with the growth rate returning to its expected value and an upward shift in the Phillips curve of an equal magnitude to the rise in the inflation rate caused by the unexpected increase in the rate of monetary expansion.

Figure 2

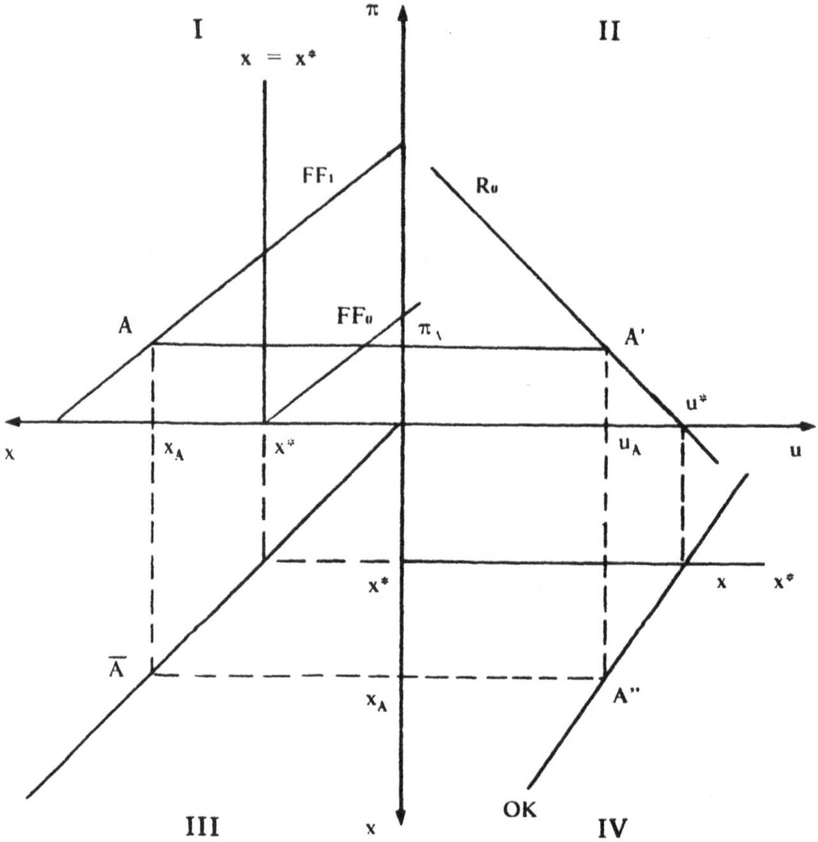

Figure 3

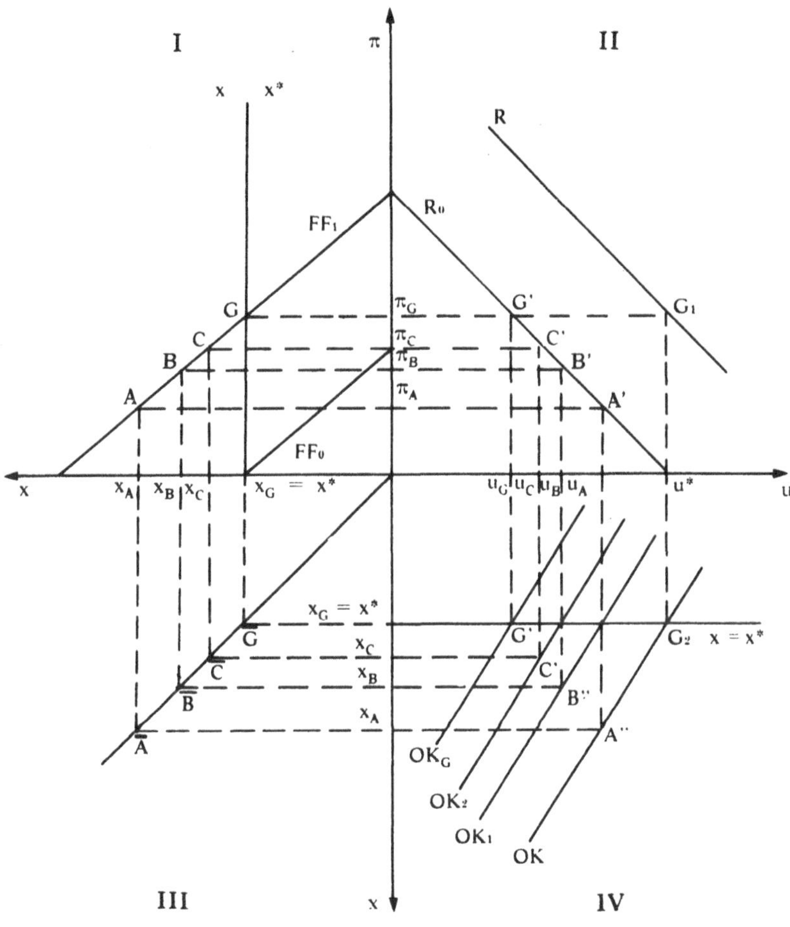
I
π
II
x
x*
R
R₀
FF₁
G
C
B
A
πG
πC
πB
πA
G'
C'
B'
A'
G₁
FF₀
x
xA
xB
xC
xG = x*
uG
uC
uB
uA
u*
u
xG = x*
G
C
B
A
xC
xB
xA
G'
C'
B''
A''
G₂
x = x*
OKG
OK₂
OK₁
OK
III
x
IV

3.1.4 *Criticisms*

Among the questionable points in this argument, it is worth paying particular attention to the neoclassical concept of labor market equilibrium, the implicit relations between monetary expansion and variations in nominal income, and the pattern of expectation formation. This last item is best left to a later stage of discussion, when other theories of inflation are analyzed. In what follows I examine the first two items.

As regards the neoclassical concept of the labor market, it is important to stress how inadequate an economic analysis is if it confines the factors determining employment to the circumscribed space of a specific market, as Keynes (1965) took pains to emphasize in his analysis of the factors determining the level of employment. Moreover, the relations between capital and labor are far more complex than those existing in a goods market. The idea that labor power is a good like any other presupposes that the labor force is homogeneous and has perfect mobility. But as Baltar tries to show, "the labor market is heterogenous and cannot be seen as a continuous space in which everyone has the same opportunities for progress in terms of earnings and conditions of employment" (Baltar 1985, 127). On the other hand, Swaelen (1982, 42) recalls that for Keynes there is no such thing as perfect mobility of the labor force, which means that there are ties between groups of workers and different industries and that transfers of workers from one industry to another involve time and costs.[14]

Presupposing two conventional curves for labor demand and labor supply, as the neoclassical analysis does, implies acceptance that all those offering and demanding on the labor market are constantly available to terminate their labor contracts and that they tend to do so as soon as market conditions change, however slightly. This is not the case, however, for to mention just one objection, firms have to pay costs whenever they hire and fire employees. They therefore tend to create barriers to prevent employees from leaving, using personnel and wage policies designed to bind an employee as closely as possible to the firm. In other words, firms strive to create close links with their employees in a way that reaches beyond the rates of pay at any given moment.[15]

Lastly, the non-existence of homogeneity and perfect mobility of the labor force leads to the recognition that the labor market is segmented and, as shown by Swaelen (1982) and Baltar (1985), that its movements should be studied bearing in mind institutional and historical factors as well. This recognition entails accepting that determinations of wages and employment cannot be boiled down to a single common logic as they are in the neoclassical analysis of the labor market, but must be analyzed separately.[16]

The second point is more controversial and lies at the heart of the monetarist innovation. This is the relationship between monetary expansion and nominal income. The monetarist argument does not establish a direct relationship between the pace of monetary expansion and the pace of price increases, as did the early exponents of the quantity theory of money. The essential point is their assertion that if the money supply expands above the expected level this will increase the speed at which nominal income rises. For this purpose, Friedman (1956) rehabilitated the quantity theory of money as a theory of demand for money. For Friedman, statements about product, nominal income, or price levels require combinations of the quantity theory of money with other specifications regarding the conditions of money supply, among other variables.

Friedman argued that his money demand theory was established using a general formulation which was capable of obtaining acceptance from a majority of economists. It was based on the assumption that money is a form of wealth[17] like any other and that each decision-making unit determines the amount of money demanded as the outcome of a process of neoclassical arbitration regarding the distribution of wealth in its various forms (money, securities, stocks, physical goods, and human capital) in such a way as to maximize the utility, in accordance with price and rate of return, of each different form of wealth. In brief, for Friedman, demand for money can be explained by a general theory of the distribution of wealth according to alternative uses, with the aim of maximizing its utility.[18] He argues that when empirical observations are matched with this theoretical framework it is possible to prove that there is a stable relation between nominal income and money supply, even though it may not necessarily be a relation of strict and permanent proportionality as it is in the conventional formulation of the quantity theory of money. In addition, Friedman set out to show that there is an asymmetrical relation between demand for money and money supply. He asserted that key factors affect the supply of money without affecting demand for it. The basic idea is that the stock of money can be controlled by the monetary authorities: "The gist of the hypothesis is that the monetary authorities have at their disposal instruments which can affect the volume of money with precision, although evidently not on a day-to-day basis" (Barbosa 1983, 70). According to Friedman, when demand for money is stable, nominal income may be highly sensitive to changes in the stock of money. In other words, for Friedman, only an increase in the stock of money can permit an increase in nominal income. Thus, as he sees it the stock of money, given its income velocity, establishes the level of nominal income.

Regarding this argument about the relation between monetary expansion and nominal income, its stability and the forms of determination, I would like to highlight three criticisms. First it is important to note Friedman's insistent refusal to accept Keynes's argument about the particularity of money because of his harmonistic conception of the capitalist system, in which there is no place for uncertainty or, as a result, for a specific demand for money, i.e., demand for liquidity.[19]

The second criticism has to do with the notion of the stability of the money demand function. According to Friedman,

> the quantity theorist need not, and generally does not, mean that the real quantity of money demanded per unit of output, or the velocity of circulation of money, is to be regarded as numerically constant over time; he does not, for example, regard it as a contradiction to the stability of the demand for money that the velocity of circulation of money rises drastically during hyperinflations. For the stability he expects is in the functional relation between the quantity of money demanded and the variables that determine it. (Friedman 1956)

In other words, for Friedman the velocity of circulation of money does not need to be constant. What is necessary is stability in the relation between the income velocity of money and a set of specific variables. His argument, in fact, is a sophisticated version of the Cambridge cash balance approach.[20] The difference is that instead of working with a fixed constant in the relation between money supply and nominal demand, Friedman and his fellow-monetarists created the view that demand for money has a stable relation to a narrow set of variables. Like all Friedman's theoretical formulations, his argument for this view is empirically based. As part of his effort to establish the idea that demand for money is a stable function, he made a point of emphasizing that statistically speaking the behavior of the money demand function is more stable than that of other economic functions which determine nominal income, such as consumption and investment. Apart from the debatable scientific validity of Friedman's empiricist argument, it must be noted that even if we accept the empiricist criterion he proposes, there will still be considerable room for doubting whether from the statistical standpoint the demand for money function is really more stable than other functions related to the components of aggregate demand: "But in fact recent empirical work has revealed great instability in both the demand for money function and the major components of the aggregate demand function and thus it is not clear that monetary policy is to be preferred to fiscal" (Pearce 1983, 283).

Finally, Friedman's argument that, in addition to an assumed stability in the relation between monetary expansion and nominal income, the former determines the latter is based on an unacceptable hypothesis regarding the exogeneity of money.[21] This hypothesis assumes that expansion of nominal income is neutral in relation to the pace of money expansion. In other words, variations in the expansion of nominal income are said not to interfere with the rate of money expansion. This type of argument is questionable in view of the fact that monetary expansion is not determined solely by the monetary authorities in some kind of entirely autonomous position regarding changes in nominal income.

The actions of monetary authorities are neither autonomous in relation to the evolution of nominal income nor, above all, the only factor determining monetary expansion. Contrary to the view emphasized with stubborn insistence by traditional textbooks of monetary theory, the expansion of purchasing power determined by the actions of banks is not a mere passive function of the deposits made by the public—deposits supposedly a function of decisions on utilization of money made by individuals based on the decisions made by monetary authorities as to the overall volume of money in an economy. Friedman's argument is deficient because it fails to recognize the capitalist nature of the banking business. Insofar as banks are loci of individual capitalist accumulation, they play an active role in the creation of purchasing power. At a time when income is expanding, the prospective profitability of banking capital changes and competition between capitalists in this field sharpens as they begin disputing those segments of the bank market which have prospects of expansion. As a result, banking capital as a whole tends to amplify money expansion and alter its pace. Thus at times when the chances of expanding banking capital become exceptionally elastic, monetary expansion accelerates significantly regardless of the decisions taken by monetary authorities. Backed by the intense mutual confidence among capitalists which periods of strong accumulation usually create, the banks create a series of instruments and norms which greatly multiply the amount of money in the economy.[22] This suggests that the pace of monetary expansion is not a determinant of but is rather determined by the expansion of nominal income, contrary to Friedman's assertions.

3.2 A Walresian Theory with Rational Expectations: New Classical Economics

As we have just seen, monetarism believes that inflation is always and everywhere a monetary phenomenon. According to this school, although in the short run an expansionary policy may cause variations in the pace at which output expands, in the long run it will bring about only an acceleration in the inflation rate. In other words, the non-neutrality of money, if possible at all, is temporary.

The debate with its most immediate adversaries began to center on how long the "short run" should be understood as lasting. For the monetarists, its duration depends directly on the size of the predictive errors made by economic agents. For the adversaries of monetarism, as long as agents could be surprised it would be possible to modify the pace of expansion of output by adopting active economic policies.

One fundamental element in this discussion was the pattern of expectations. Until the late 1960s, models of expectation formation were based on the principle that expectations were adjusted in an adaptive way. The adaptive expectation model was suggested by Cagen (1956). Basically it proposed that mistaken expectations are always partially corrected. Thus a positive fraction of any error made is added to new predictions:

$$P(t+1) - P'(t) = a \cdot (P(t) - P'(t)) \tag{8}$$

where:

- $P'(t)$ is the expected value of the variable P at $t-1$ in relation to the period t;
- $P(t)$ is the actual value of the variable P at time t;
- a is the adjustment coefficient $(0 < a < 1)$.

By manipulation of expression (8) it is possible to conclude that the predicted value of P can be understood, according to this method, as a mere weighted average of its present value and the latest prediction. However, the latest prediction can also be understood as a weighted average, in this case, of the latest actual value in the penultimate prediction. If this line of reasoning is used recurrently, the adaptive expectation method suggests that the best predictor of a future value is a linear combination of all its past values with decreasing weights, as shown in this formula deduced from expression (8):

$$P'(t+1) = a \cdot P(t) + a \cdot (1-a) \cdot P(t-1) + a \cdot (1-a)^2 \cdot P(t-2) + \ldots + a \cdot (1-a)^n \cdot P(t-n) + \ldots \tag{9}$$

This method assumes the hypothesis that economic agents form their expectations by taking only the past into account and does not consider such information as drastic changes in economic policy.

3.2.1 *The Axiom of Rationality and the Hypothesis of Rational Expectations*

The end of the 1960s coincided with the crisis of the neoclassical synthesis as a paradigm of economic analysis in general and inflation analysis in particular, based on the well-known Phillips curve. The fundamental critique of this paradigm, which arose when its empirical inadequacy had been demonstrated by the advent of stagflation, was methodological. The focus was the theoretical incompatibility between the neoclassical microeconomic foundations of the paradigm and the analysis of the underuse of resources created by its macro side:

> As an academic and professional discipline, economics lives with a fundamental internal contradiction: what is taught in conventional microeconomics is incompatible with what is taught in macroeconomics. In the former, every market is a price-auction market that clears based on competitive bidding within a framework of supply and demand. Accordingly, any market is always in equilibrium, having no unsatisfied bidders, and every individual is a maximizer in his decisions to consume and produce. Macroeconomics, on the other hand, is basically the study of markets that do not clear and are not in equilibrium. (Thurow 1983, 4)

As a result, economic theory has moved in recent times toward an attempt to eliminate the theoretical incompatibility in question by means of a detailed study of the microfoundations of the main contributors to economic analysis, using such a study as a basis for the reconstruction of a consistent analytical whole with which it will then be possible to understand contemporary macroeconomic phenomena.[23]

One influential example of these various approaches to eliminating this methodological incompatibility is "neoclassicized" macroeconomics, i.e, the attempt to rethink macroeconomics using neoclassical microfoundations. From this perspective it was necessary to question all analytical procedures to make them compatible with the basic axioms of neoclassical theory. The main axiom, of course, is the rationality of economic agents. This led to rejection of the adaptive expectation model because it was seen to be inconsistent with such an axiom. Why should economic agents make use only of information on the past when forming their expectations? How could a rational economic agent make systematic mistakes? These were the key questions challenging and, indeed, negating the adaptive expectation model from the standpoint of the new developments in economic theory. As a result, in the 1970s the hypothesis of rational expectations became more and more widely accepted:

> Rational expectations also assume that individual decision makers learn rationally rather than adaptively. This means that they do not gradually change their behavior in response to new pieces of information or different circumstances but quickly and discontinuously adopt new decision rules. People are also assumed to look to the future, their expectations, rather than to the past, their experience, in making decisions. The emphasis on rational, as opposed to adaptive, behavior makes the valid point that man, being a thinking animal, tries to learn from his past and not repeat his mistakes. Behavior is sometimes going to change quickly and discontinuously. Accordingly, any theory which assumes only gradual change in behavior, adaptive expectations, is obviously wrong. (Thurow 1984, 156)

The original idea was put forward by John Muth in 1961: "He suggested that, in the context of a model, expectations of individuals are rational when they are identical with the predictions of that model" (Klamer 1984, 11). This observation served as a basis for many economists' work in the 1970s; led by Robert Lucas, Thomas Sargent, and Neil Wallace, they consolidated an approach which has now become known as new classical economics.

3.2.2 *The New Classical Model and its General Implications*

As Klamer points out, new classical economics is not the same thing as the rational expectations hypothesis, although this is its main contribution and its most salient characteristic:

> Rational expectations and new classical economics are commonly taken as synonyms, but this interpretation is probably incorrect. Rational expectations does not necessarily separate new classical economists from others. The policy ineffectiveness proposition and the issue of equilibrium modeling have turned out to be more controversial. (Klamer 1984, 13)

What characterizes new classical economics is the combination of the rational expectations hypothesis with the basic axioms of neoclassical theory—specifically, the principle that economic agents seek to maximize utility and profits, and the idea of "efficient market clearing".

Unlike their neoclassical predecessors, the new classical economists do not assume that information is perfect. This is the point distinguishing them from the pre-Keynesian view. Instead of using the idea of perfect information, they argue that economic agents use all the information available and seek out new information until the marginal cost of acquiring and processing such information equals the marginal benefit derived therefrom. Hence the new classical concept of equilibrium is different from the classical concept. Whereas classical economists thought that only one solution was possible for the system, the new classical school says various equilibria are possible, depending on the entire universe of information available.

The new classical economists took this conceptual structure as a premise for constructing a theory to serve as an alternative to Keynesian theory in that variations in output would not be explained by variations in effective demand. The basic points underlying their explanation are that economic agents are rational and a repetitive conception of the economic process. Since economic agents are rational and hence unlikely to make systematic mistakes, they tend to approximate the correct model of the economic structure.

This conclusion has important implications for an analysis of the effectiveness of economic policies. Given that rational expectation theorists assume that the information available to economic policy makers is no better on average than that available to decision makers in the private sector, economic agents' tendency to interpret the economy correctly makes it perfectly possible to foresee the consequences of all economic policy decisions, however remote they may be. This anticipation of the effects of economic policy means in practice that they are neutralized. In fact, this anticipation goes still further, as when economic agents systematically analyze the economic situation they tend to anticipate economic policy decisions themselves and neutralize those decisions even before they are implemented:

> If public policy makers use certain types of econometric models to forecast economic events and then intervene in the economy on the basis of such forecasts, the private economic actors know that is what the public policy makers are going to do. When investors make their private decisions, they make them with the understanding that government will intervene in the economy under certain circumstances. As a result, an actual decision to intervene will have no *new* impact on private decisions. The impact of the intervention has already been built into the initial decisions on an expected value basis. (Thurow 1983, 160)

The consequence of this process is the ineffectiveness of economic policy.[24] This means that no economic policy can have a real impact unless it is totally unexpected. Any policy decision of a systematic kind can perfectly well be foreseen and neutralized when economic agents form their expectations rationally. Hence to have a real effect economic policy must be random. Only a stochastic shock can take the economic agents by surprise, induce them to make mistakes, and thus lead to variations away from the previous equilibrium.

From this foundation new classical theory moves on to conclude that variations in production and employment must be understood as variations of a stochastic nature, producible solely by deficiencies in the information system or directly by random shocks. Thus models used in macroeconomic analysis should include in equations representing the various relations of equilibrium an error element μ whose mathematical expectation is equal to zero: $E(\mu) = 0$.[25]

3.2.3 *The End of Short-term Non-neutrality of Money and the Direct Relation between Monetary Growth and Inflation*

The new classical approach leads to a more radical conclusion than that put forward by the monetarists. The latter argued that money may be non-neutral but only for the short term. This temporary possibility of real effects resulting from monetary administration, however, is refuted by the new classical economists. In their view economic agents bring the acceleration factor into effect as soon as they realize that government is creating the conditions for a change in the pace of monetary growth. Thus forecast inflation is no longer a simple weighted average of past inflations, as in the adaptive expectation model, but a direct function of predictions about the rate of growth in the supply of money over and above real economic growth, plus an element of error:

(a) inflation expectation according to the adaptive expectation hypothesis:

$$P'(t+1) = f(P(t-n), a) \tag{10}$$

where:

$n = 0, 1, 2, \ldots$
a is the adaptation coefficient ($0 < a < 1$);

(b) inflation expectation according to the rational expectation hypothesis:

$$P'(t+1) = E(p/I(t)) \tag{11}$$

where:

$E(p/I(t))$ is the optimal expectation at t conditioned by the information available at that moment.

If all the new classical assumptions are taken into account, this function takes on a specific shape:[26]

$$P'(t+1) = E(p/I(t)) = E(m/I(t)) - x^* \tag{12}$$

where:

$E(m/I(t)$ is the optimal expectation regarding the expansion of the money supply at time $t+1$, conditioned by the information available at t;

x^* is the trend rate of real economic growth.

Thus forecast inflation should be equal to the difference between the expected rate of growth in the money supply in view of all the information available at time t and the rate of real economic growth. If for whatever reason it is expected that the government will step up the rate of monetary expansion, the new classical model indicates an expectation of immediate and proportional acceleration in the inflation rate.

For the new classical economists, inflation usually follows the model:

$$P(t+1) = P'(t+1) + e_1 \tag{13}$$

where:

e_1 is a stochastic variable with $E(e_1) = 0$

and given the previous expression for $P'(t+1)$, the following is obtained for the basic new classical model:

$$P(t+1) = E(m/I(t)) - x^* + a \cdot H(t+1) + e_1 \tag{14}$$

where:

$H(t+1)$ is the expectational error in the prediction of change in the money supply at time t, with a partial effect on inflation, similarly to the monetarist model of inflation examined above.

Thus the new classical model of inflation suggests that the rate of inflation follows an identical course to that of the expected rate of expansion of the money supply, minus the real rate of economic growth and the expectational errors made in forecasting monetary expansion and immediate stochastic shocks. As I shall show later, this formulation is one of the alternatives on which to base the inertial interpretation of inflationary trends in view of the inertia which monetary expansion assumes in some economies.

3.2.4 *Some Criticisms*

All the criticisms already made with regard to the monetarist model also apply here, since the same model is assumed as relevant by the new classical school. The main problems are the doubtful hypothesis that markets can adjust perfectly through price variation, the idea of a labor market in which employers hire labor according to the value of its marginal productivity, and the idea that the money supply is exogenously determined and regulates nominal income.

Furthermore, the whole set of hypotheses subsumed in the notion of rational expectations is highly restrictive with regard to the actual behavior of economic agents, thus making its results even more debatable. One striking aspect of this restrictiveness is that rational expectationists assume economic agents to behave in a very special manner. As Simonsen nicely puts it:

> Rational expectation models not only assume that a set of linear equations links the endogenous and exogenous variables together; they also affirm that economic agents know these equations and believe in them. This is the Achilles heel of such theories. (Simonsen 1983, 447)

The idea underlying Simonsen's skepticism (but not fully developed by him) is that it is impossible for a single model of the economy to be collectively approximated. It is not hard to see why.

The first reason is that an economic system is not repetitive, as assumed by new classical theory, and therefore economic agents cannot be said to converge toward the correct model of the economic structure. The idea of an economy behaving repetitively presupposes the dubious notion of a stable economic system[27] and of ahistorical economies. Economic systems are in permanent revolution, and this is one of the forces which always distinguishes competitive approaches to economic analysis. Moreover, when it is a capitalist economy that is under discussion, the various economic actors cannot be understood as a single homogeneous unit. Hence the differences between the various approaches to economic analysis tend to depend on the position and the scope of action of each economic actor. Finally, as Keynes set out to demonstrate, expectations are formed under conditions of uncertainty; they are very different from something which could be calculated through a probabilistic process of statistical inference. Later on I shall return to this point when I introduce the idea of Conditioned Expectations.[28]

3.3 A Marshall-Kaleckian Theory with Conditioned Expectations and the Concept of a Stable Economy: Neostructuralism

The importance of this school flows from two mutually related aspects. First it played an important role in disseminating the hypothesis of the inertial tendency of the inflationary process which has inspired recent heterodox programs of economic stabilization implemented in several countries. Secondly, this school has occupied an increasingly central position in the economic debate, especially in the developing countries where it is seen as offering an alternative to conventional analysis. Among other things, the neostructuralist approach has shown how ineffective and problematical monetarist stabilization policies are.[29]

According to Taylor (1983), neostructuralist macroeconomics is characterized by the fact that it takes the economic structure as an element of real importance in the construction of a theory; the features differentiating economic sectors and, above all, the roles and positions of the various economic agents are recognized as such, rather than being boiled down into a single homogeneous category.[30] In other words, neostructuralism analyzes the economy from a perspective which differs from that of conventional approaches. The basic idea is that an economy should be analyzed not only through its general macroeconomic relations but also by taking into account the specific characteristics of and relations among the various sectors and classes in a given economic structure.

3.3.1 *Conflict over Distribution*

As a result of this theoretical approach the neostructuralists have a very different view of the inflationary process, which they see as resulting from a conflict over distribution: "Inflation is a sign that a capitalist economy is trying to sweep class conflict over distribution of product under the rug" (Taylor 1983, 205). In the short run workers and employers do not accept a reduction in their share of income, so that the markup remains constant and inflation therefore keeps pace with costs. In the long run, when, according to this school, the economy is operating at full production capacity,[31] the acceleration of inflation through an increase in markups is the means the economy finds to achieve the forced savings required for increasing the growth rate above the level associated with full utilization of production capacity. It is worth examining this argument in more detail, using a schematic outline of neostructuralist thinking to obtain a clearer insight into the dynamics of conflict over distribution and its consequences.

The first point to be singled out clearly provides a sharp contrast to conventional economic theory: for the neostructuralists there are two basic classes with contradictory objectives in capitalism. The minimum objective of the workers is to prevent their real income from diminishing. Real income is equal to the nominal wage divided by a price index which derived from the typical working-class pattern of consumption:

$$w_r = w/(a \cdot P_L + b \cdot P_I) \qquad (15)$$

where:

- w_r is the real wage;
- w is the nominal wage;
- P_L is the flexprice level;[32]
- P_I is the fixprice level;
- a is the proportion of flexpriced products in the workers' consumption basket;
- b is the proportion of fixpriced products in the workers' consumption basket.

If the prices of the flexpriced products consumed by workers rise, there is a reduction in real wages which sooner or later workers will counteract by demanding a rise in their nominal wages. However, this affects the objective of capitalists in the fixprice sector. According to Taylor (1983), prices in this sector are formed by the following markup rule:

$$P = (1 + z) \cdot (w \cdot b^* + e \cdot P_0{}^* \cdot a_0) \qquad (16)$$

where:

P is the price fixed by the producer of a fixpriced product;
z is the markup rate;
w is the nominal wage;
b^* is the labor coefficient per product;[33]
e is the exchange rate;
P_0 is the price in foreign currency of imported inputs;
a_0 is the coefficient of utilization of imported inputs per unit of output.

If this expression is taken in total values, i.e., if both sides are multiplied by the sales volume x and gross profit is isolated, the following expression for the profit rate is easily arrived at:[34]

$$r = u \cdot z/(1 + z) \tag{17}$$

where:

r is the profit rate;
u is the level of utilization of productive capacity.

Thus the profit rate is a function of the markup and of the level of capacity utilization. So if nominal wages rise and if it is not possible to increase the level of capacity utilized, it follows that the profit rate must decrease when the markup decreases, provided that prices remain unchanged. This can be seen from equation 18, which is an elementary transformation of equation 16:

$$z = P/(w \cdot b^* + e \cdot P_0{}^* \cdot a_0) - 1. \tag{18}$$

For the profit rate to remain constant, prices in the fixprice sector must also increase. But these prices affect the cost of the workers' basket of staples, which in turn brings renewed pressure for a wage rise, and this leads to another round of increases in the fixprice sector. The whole process tends to be convergent if the desired markups and real wages are stable. Figure 4 shows the interactions between the three conditions which synthesize the reactions of firms in the fixprice sector to wage rises and the reactions of workers to rises in flexprices and fixprices, in view of an initial rise P_I in flexprices (assuming stability of desired markups and real wages). In algebraic terms, these conditions can be expressed as follows:

$$\Delta w = w_r \cdot a \cdot \Delta P_L \quad (19)$$

$$\Delta P_I = (1 + z) \cdot (\Delta w \cdot b^*) \quad (20)$$

$$\Delta w = w \cdot b \cdot \Delta P_I \quad (21)$$

where:

Δw is the absolute variation in nominal wages;
ΔP_L is the absolute variation in flexprices;
ΔP_I is the absolute variation in fixprices.

Three points of this analysis must be highlighted. First, a minor shock in prices in the flexprice sector, combined with workers' resistance to a reduction in their real income and that of employers to a reduction in their profit rate, leads to a recurrent rise in prices in the fixprice sector. Second, this process is convergent owing to the stability of desired markups and real wages, and owing to the non-reaction of flexprices. Third—and here we come to one of the contributions of the structuralist analysis—shocks from the flexprice sector are recurrent in developing economies.[35]

It is also important to stress that conflict again appears as the expression of a movement triggered by capitalists to attempt to push up the rate of accumulation, or (seen from a different angle) to raise the profit rate. As equation 17 shows, the profit rate is a direct function of the level of capacity utilization and of the markup. When capacity is fully utilized, according to the neostructuralist argument, the profit rate can be increased only if markups are increased; this occurs through a reduction in real wages, provided that the other factors in equation 18 are kept constant (see figure 5). The neostructuralists argue that while idle capacity exists, growth can be accelerated without adversely affecting real wages, but when capacity is fully utilized the accumulation rate can be raised only through forced saving on the part of workers, with a reduction in real wages on the one hand and an increase in markups on the other. These relations are synthetically shown in figure 5, which presents the necessary conditions for matching the alternative rates of growth in the capital stock (g) with the basic equilibrium identity established between investment and saving, which in Taylor's formulation appears as the resultant of the following system:[36]

Figure 4

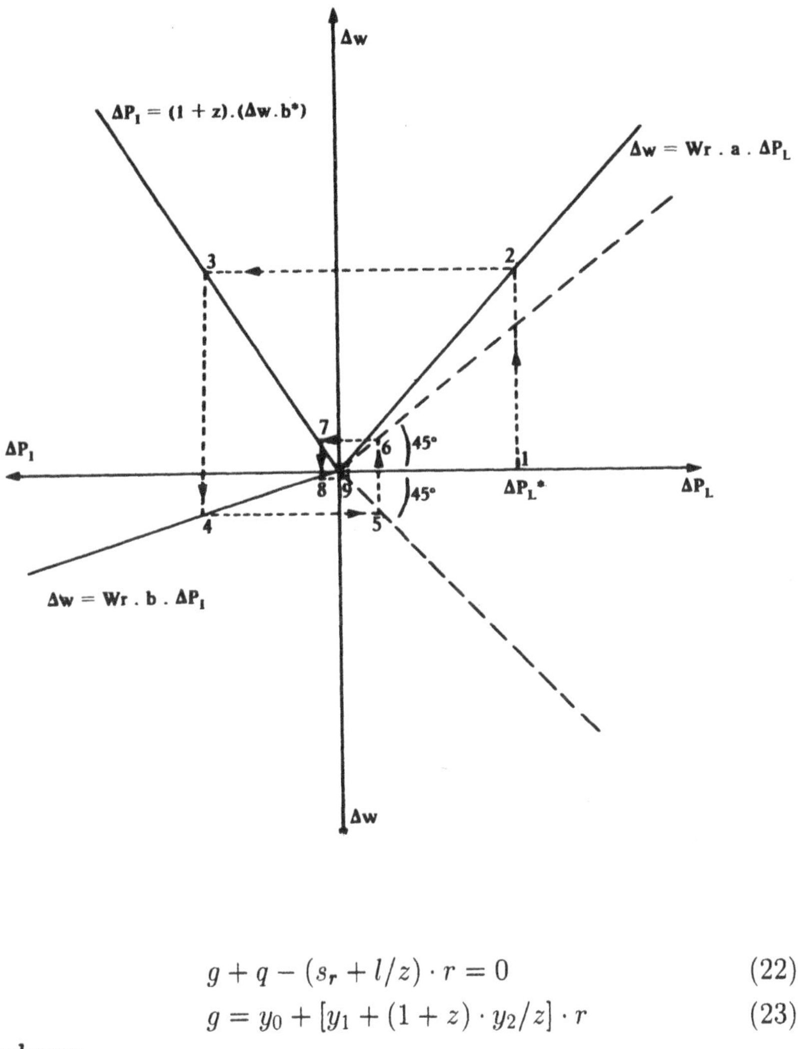

$$g + q - (s_r + l/z) \cdot r = 0 \tag{22}$$

$$g = y_0 + [y_1 + (1 + z) \cdot y_2/z] \cdot r \tag{23}$$

where:

- g is the rate of growth of the stock of capital;
- q is the relation between exports and capital stock;
- l is the proportion of the cost of imported inputs in the overall variable cost;
- s_r is the capitalists' saving rate;

y_0 is the investment which does not depend on current conditions in the economy but reflects the "animal spirits" of the management of public and private enterprises;
y_1 is the acceleration coefficient of the investments that depend on the profit rate;
y_2 is the acceleration coefficient of the investments that depend on the level of capacity utilization.

Thus an acceleration in the rate of growth beyond a certain limit is possible only by means of an acceleration of inflation and a reduction of real wages. If this occurs, however, countervailing forces tend to arise. In other words, the situation is potentially unstable. With a rising accumulation rate, full utilization of production capacity, mounting pressure for new jobs, and inflation, it is possible that workers will gain strength and force a recovery—or even an increase—in real wages. According to the neostructuralists this would mean a reduction of the profit rate—in accordance with equations 3 and 4—and a reduction of investment, given the investment function implicit in equation 23. This is the theoretical basis for the neostructuralists' view of inflationary processes and business cycles. As Taylor himself sums it up:

> The result in the medium run is the business cycle, and in the longer run a fair stability in the functional income distribution. The cyclical picture is as follows: an investment boom in the first instance shifts the income distribution toward capital through forced saving. But as employment rises or inflation speeds up, labor gains strength and forces an increase in the real wage. Profit rates fall, investment stagnates, and output growth declines. Wage claims then erode, the distribution shifts toward profits, and the stage is set for another upswing. (Taylor 1983, 205)

In short, according to the neostructuralist analysis, capitalist economies are characterized by permanent conflict which tends to lead them to recurrent oscillations, associated with spurts of accelerated inflation. To minimize the inherent costs of such processes, capitalists seek to negotiate contracts which will ensure more stable relations between capital and labor.

Figure 5

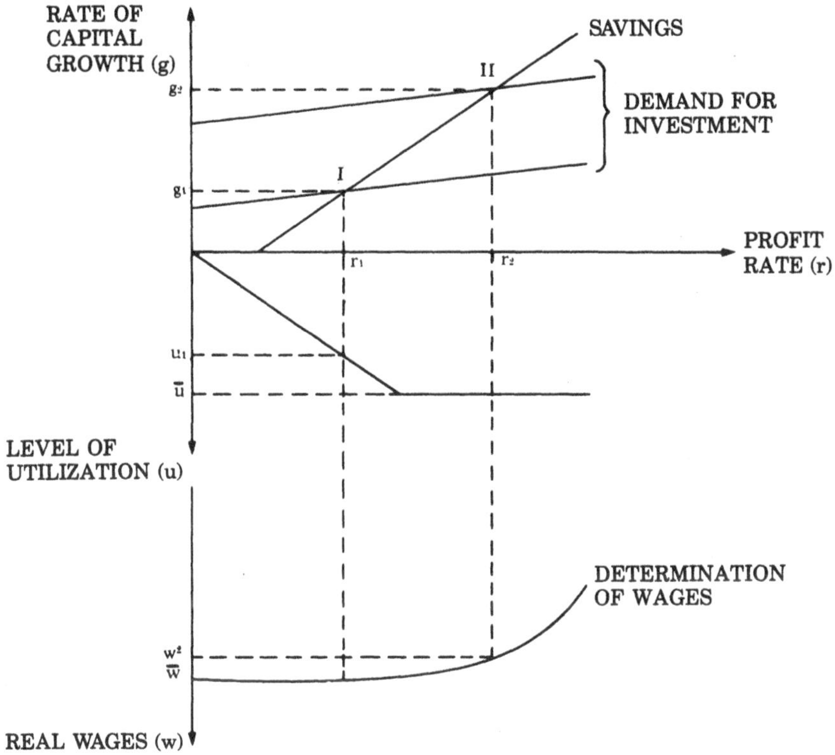

MACRO EQUILIBRIUM WITH CLEARING BY CAPACITY UTILIZATION (Point I) AND CLEARING BY FORCED SAVING (Point II)

3.3.2 *Chronically Inflationary Economies and Wage Indexation*

All capitalist economies tend to be subject to conflict and to inflation, but these tendencies become still more pronounced in the developing countries. As the structuralists point out, developing economies are submitted to strong recurrent pressure for changes in relative prices, and as a result they tend to be chronically inflationary. Hence the contractual relations inherent to capitalist societies tend to assume specific forms in developing economies. As Frenkel (1986) concludes after an examination of research findings from five countries with chronically inflationary economies (Argentina, Brazil, Chile, Colombia, and Costa Rica), there is a tendency for wages to be indexed to a cost-of-living index: "The most general conclusion to be derived from the research findings described is that in processes of high inflation, indexing to past inflation is the normal form used to make periodic adjustments to nominal wages paid to employees" (Frenkel 1986, 34). Frenkel also concludes that this particular form of contract can become "the normal form used to make periodic adjustments to nominal wages paid to employees" because this is the best way of minimizing conflicts and costs in relations between capital and labor in chronically inflationary economies. The conclusion is made clear in three passages. The first states that "wages result from implicit contracts which attempt to minimize workers' and employers' costs of procurement, information and transaction, and to stabilize labor relations." Later Frenkel adds: "If the norm is directed to minimizing conflicts and stabilizing social relations, it must be based on generally available information which can reasonably be appealed to as objective." Finally he turns to the objections of those who defend the rational expectations hypothesis against the indexation argument and offers the following critique:

> In this sense it becomes somewhat ingenuous to argue as is customary among those who advocate rational expectations. This argument contends that indexing to past inflation assumes that agents are systematically myopic or irrational, since it implies that agents always expect future inflation rates equal to past rates. If this subject is considered in the light of

> broader conditioning factors, such as those mentioned above, and if the costs of information and conflict are taken into account, it seems reasonable to believe that the latter counterbalance the possible costs resulting from a future inflation rate above or below the preceding rate (particularly in a process of high inflation), and it therefore becomes clear that indexation is far from being irrational behavior. (Frenkel 1986, 40)

In short, in a chronically inflationary environment, the cost of obtaining information and the cost of conflict are very high and one way of minimizing them is to index labor contracts to a cost-of-living indicator.

3.3.3 *Wage Indexation, Inertia, and the Components and Determinants of Inflation*

The perception of the tendency for wages to be indexed to inflation is the basis for development of the neostructuralist hypothesis of the inertial tendency of inflation in chronically inflationary economies.[37] Bacha (1982) takes as his starting-point the idea that in a capitalist economy prices tend to be formed in accordance with an equation similar to expression 16:

$$P = z \cdot (w \cdot b + e \cdot x_i \cdot j_i) \tag{24}$$

where:

- P is the price;
- z is the markup force (1+ proportional profit margin on variable costs);
- w is the nominal wage;
- b is the inverse of labor productivity;
- e is the exchange rate;
- x_i is the dollar price of imported components;
- j_i is the consumption coefficient of imported inputs per unit of output.

If nominal wages are indexed and if the exchange rate is adjusted through a system of mini-devaluations that continually maintains a given parity between the national currency and the dollar, and assuming that parameters b and j are constant, parity is fixed, the real wage is at a peak, and wage resistance is a given coefficient (related to the frequency of pay adjustments), Bacha shows that the rates of variation of prices, wages, and exchange rates can be expressed as follows:

$$\hat{P} = \hat{z} + l\hat{w} + (\hat{1} - l) \cdot (\hat{e} + \hat{x}_i) \tag{25}$$

$$\hat{w} = h \cdot \hat{P} + (1 - h) \cdot \hat{P}_1 \tag{26}$$

$$\hat{e} = \hat{P} - \hat{x} \tag{27}$$

where:

ˆ indicates that the variable is expressed in terms of its variation over time;
l is the relation $z \cdot w \cdot b/P$;
h is the wage resistance coefficient;
x is the price level in dollars.

Bacha argues that although the markup is fixed in the short run, it may vary in the long run because of the excess demand which would occur if the desired growth exceeded the conditions for equilibrium between saving and investment, as we saw from Taylor's argument (summed up in figure 5). To represent this, Bacha suggests a linear relation between markup and capacity utilization:

$$\hat{z} = m \cdot (u - 1) \tag{28}$$

where:

m is the adjustment velocity ($m > 0$);
u is the level of capacity utilization ($u = 1$ indicates normal level of operation).

In view of this equation and of equations 25, 26, and 27, Bacha presents a complete expression for the price variation rate:

$$\hat{P} = \hat{P}_{-1} + m \cdot (u - 1) \cdot (1 - h) + (\hat{x}_i - \hat{x}) \cdot (1 - l)/l \cdot (1 - h). \tag{29}$$

This expression divides the price variation rate into three components, according to Simonsen's classification (1970):

> Past inflation is the 'feedback component'; the utilization level function is the 'demand regulation component'; the difference between the rate at which prices of imported inputs increase

> and the dollar inflation rate is the 'autonomous component'—which in this case can also be called the imported inflation component or external shock. (Bacha 1982, 177)

Thus, when the demand regulation component and the external shock are nil—that is, if $u = 1$ and $\hat{x}_i = \hat{x}$—expression 29 indicates that inflation will be equal to past inflation. Under these circumstances, then, inflation is neither more nor less than its inertial tendency.[38] This, in essence, is the argument for the inertial tendency of inflation.[39] In the absence of external shocks (in the strict sense or in that of demand regulation), the dynamics of inflation is confined to a repetition of past inflationary behavior.

In addition to the above hypotheses, neostructuralism attempted to explain the inflation rate in a way that can help to understand better the type of stabilization policy inspired by this school. As Bacha puts it, the need to provide such an explanation is perceived in the following manner: "When $u = 1$ and $\hat{x}_i = \hat{x}$, all equation (29) says is that present inflation is equal to past inflation, but how the value of this rate of inflation equilibrium is determined is a question that is not answerable from the arguments developed so far" (Bacha 1982, 177).

To answer this question, neostructuralism starts with the idea that open economies revolve around a center of gravity established by the convergence of two basic relations of equilibrium: external equilibrium and internal equilibrium.[40]

According to Lance Taylor, an open economy must be adjusted in such a way as to satisfy two equilibria:

> 1. The trade deficit (foreign saving) must equal investment minus national saving. 2. The trade deficit must also equal the sum of imports (capital, intermediate and consumer goods) and net interest payments on debt, minus exports and other net current foreign exchange receipts such as emigrant remittances. (Taylor 1983, 6)

In Bacha's formulation these conditions mean that, given certain macroeconomic parameters, an economy will not be stable unless it presents a specific pairing of price increases (P) and growth in potential output (Y_k). To prove this, he first shows that the basic identities of external and internal

Figure 6

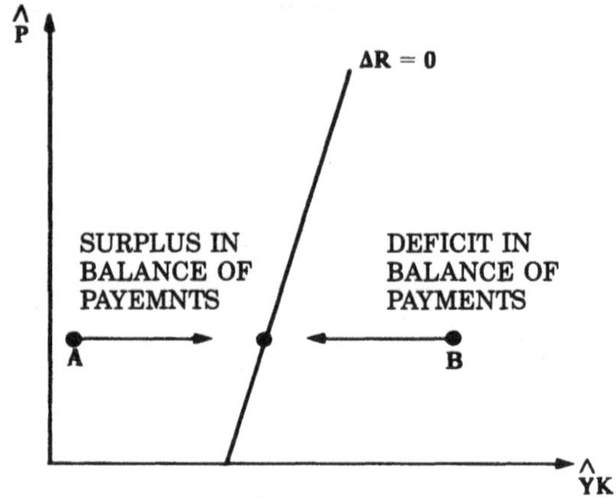

Figure 7

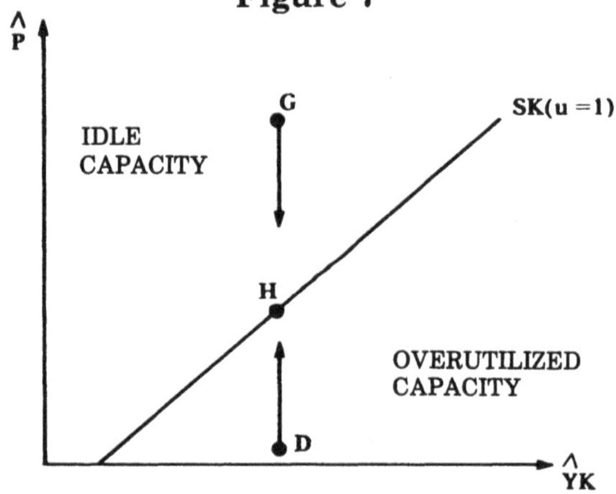

Figure 8

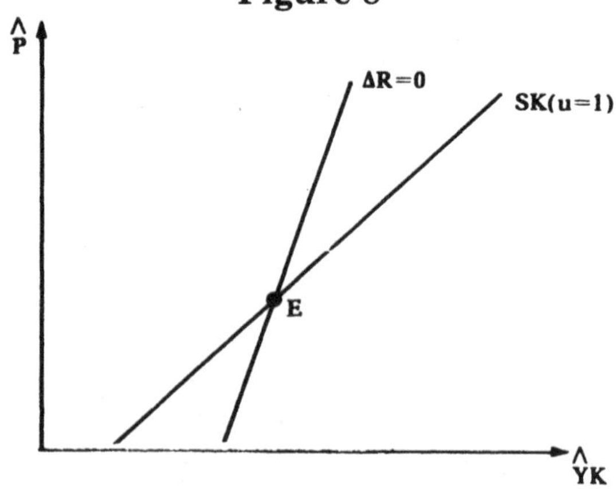

equilibria can be represented by curves that establish direct relations between rates of price increase and rates of growth of potential output.

Figures 6 and 7 show these two relationships. In figure 6, curve $\triangle R = 0$ indicates the pairs of rates of growth in potential output and rates of inflation which satisfy the condition of external equilibrium. In figure 7 curve SK indicates the pairs of rates of growth in potential output and rates of inflation corresponding to the possible situations of internal equilibrium.[41] Points outside these curves represent unstable situations.[42] On external equilibrium, Bacha says:

> Let us consider an economy which in the short run is operating at point B in Figure 6, admitting for the moment that the inflation rate is an exogenous factor. If this point lies to the right of $\triangle R = 0$, there will be a balance of payments deficit and the economy will therefore be continuously losing its international reserves. This position is not sustainable in the medium run. Two things can happen. On the one hand the drain on foreign exchange corresponds to a mopping-up of the internal mass of money supply. Unless the Central Bank promotes a counterbalancing expansion in internal credit, there will be a generalized shortage of liquidity, and sooner or later this will cause a reduction in the rate of private investment. (Bacha 1982, 175)

Similarly, Bacha argues that situations represented by points outside curve SK in figure 7 correspond to situations of instability: "Points beneath SK are positions of overutilized capacity, where inflation will therefore be accelerating. Points above SK indicate situations of idle capacity, for which inflation will therefore be decelerating" (Bacha 1982). In other words, adjustment to curve SK occurs through acceleration or deceleration of the inflation rate, while situations of external disequilibrium are solved by an acceleration or deceleration in the expansion of potential output. Given the fact that the two curves have different slopes,[43] there is only one point (E in figure 8), i.e., a single pair of rates of growth in potential output and inflation that permits a corresponding stability in the conditions for general equilibrium (internal and external).[44]

3.3.4 *Other Explanations for the Inertia of Inflation*

Before commenting on the importance and limitations of neostructuralist thinking on the question of inflation, I want to note briefly the fact that there are alternative explanations for the inertial tendency of inflation. In addition to Frenkel's argument, which provides a theoretical foundation for the institutionalization of wage indexing, there are two further explanations, one inspired by new classicism and another based on game theory.

As we have seen, the new classical model suggests that inflation is equal to the expected monetary expansion plus two components, one related to errors in forecasts of monetary expansion and the other to stochastic shocks. The best projection of inflation corresponds to the projection of monetary expansion minus the expected rate of real growth. This is the basic conclusion of the new classical model. When the best projection of incremental monetary expansion in relation to the expected rate of real growth is past inflation, then inflation becomes inertial.[45] Strictly speaking this is an explanation of the non-inertial nature of the momentum of inflation, or in other words an explanation of the reproduction of inflation rates on the basis of governmental inertia:

> An alternative 'rational expectations' view denies that there is any inherent momentum in the present process of inflation. This view maintains that firms and workers have come now to expect high rates of inflation in the future and that they strike inflationary bargains in the light of that expectation. However, it is held that people expected high inflation in the future precisely because the government's current and prospective monetary and fiscal policies warrant those expectations. (Sargent 1982)

The other explanation for the inertial tendency is inspired by Tobin and based on game theory. The basic idea is that inertia results from what might be called "strategic interdependence among private agents":

> In fact, rational individual behavior, besides depending on anticipated economic policies, also depends on the other individuals' decisions. Moreover, economic agents must take their own decisions without knowing how other players will act, which

> brings inflation theory into the field of games with imperfect information. Rational expectations literature explicitly recognizes the problems of strategic interdependence between the private sector and the government, activism meaning that the government decides to act as a dominant Stackelberg player. But, as noted by Tobin, this literature plainly ignores that, except in auction markets, there is no sense in treating the private sector as a single player. Summing up, the central weakness of the rational expectations macroeconomics is to describe as a two-person game what actually should be analyzed as an $n+1$ person game. Tobin correctly guessed that, if price-setting games were appropriately discussed in terms of strategic interdependence, inertia would emerge as a powerful inflationary force. (Simonsen 1986)[46]

Tobin's basic idea (1981) is that inertia results from the fact that economic agents tend to follow an inertial pattern of price adjustment so as to minimize the risks they face. In a context where decisions are uncoordinated, agents tend to adopt such behavior because the net expected loss should the velocity of price increases turn out to be slower than that forecast by the majority of agents would be greater than the net loss incurred should prices go up even faster than the majority expect:

> More accurately, it is an $n+1$-person game, with the n private groups playing mainly against each other. Each is interested in its volume of employment or sales, to be sure, but also in its real wage or price relative to those of other groups. Your line of least resistance, of apparently least risk, is to follow the inertial pattern, expecting everyone else to do likewise. The result—assuming the government means business—is generally low volume but no loss of relative status. And if others do disinflate, you will gain in real income and relative position and lose less in volume. On the other hand, if you disinflate without assurance that others will do likewise, you risk great loss of real income and status for what will likely be a small gain of volume. (Tobin 1981, 26)

3.3.5 *The Importance and Limits of Neostructuralist Analysis*

There is no doubt that the hypothesis of an inertial trend in chronically inflationary economies was an important contribution from neostructuralist thinking, which thereby gave a definitive demonstration of the problems associated with orthodox stabilization policies.[47] But neostructuralism has not developed a theory which can give a real understanding of the contemporary inflationary process in all its plenitude.

To put my meaning more clearly, neostructuralism suggests that inflation has two components, a shock component and a tendential one. Shocks are understood as exogenous movements to be analyzed ad hoc.[48] This conclusion derives in my view from the fact that a stable conception of the economic structure is assumed. Such a conception is implicit in the basic pricing model used in neostructuralist analysis. This assertion is justified in what follows.

The idea that markups are fixed in the short run but vary in the medium run only with excess demand seems debatable. The process whereby firms determine prices has had an important role in the acceleration of inflation, bearing in mind the present conditions of capitalism,[49] particularly in economies undergoing adjustment.

The basic problem with neostructuralism as far as this question is concerned is that it works with an assumption of "normal prices". But to assume normal prices is to some extent to assume that the economy has a stable structure. Accepting the hypothesis of normal prices would mean assuming that firms have the expectation that costs tend to vary around predictable figures and that sales volumes tend to oscillate around a preplanned production level. It is basically assumed that the economy is operating under conditions of stability. More detail on this point is given in the ensuing paragraphs.

Models of normal prices are based on the idea that prices are formed according to a simple rule of fixed markup, and consequently that capitalist firms merely pass their own costs on. Such conditions of normality are said to derive from the fact that in periods of stability capitalists are confident of the occurrence of relatively small oscillations converging around a predictable level of demand. They also expect costs to present a variation coefficient considered insignificant around an equally predictable trend. These expectations, it is argued, justify belief in an average sales volume for long enough to guarantee in the medium run an adequate level of return on the capital invested,[50] while also permitting the establishment of stable contracts to govern labor relations, supplies, and credit.[51] Under these conditions, inflation depends only on the pace at which costs increase, and in the absence of inflationary shocks this pace, in turn, is a direct outcome of past inflation (in the case of countries with chronic inflation).

Aside from the questionable assumption about the existence of automatic clearing mechanisms which can guarantee a normal level of capacity utilization—particularly debatable under conditions of adjustment—it must be stressed that the normal costs assumption is highly problematic under present conditions. This issue is discussed by Tavares and Belluzzo (1986), for whom the model of normal prices is based on the idea that prices are defined such that they have a stable relationship to costs (fixed markup). Given that production takes time, prices could be planned in this way only if it were possible to have prior knowledge of the costs that will prevail during the production period, which in turn presupposes the possibility of concluding stable labor, supply, and credit contracts. It is possible to imagine the feasibility of stable labor contracts, but contemporary capitalism makes it difficult to reach stable supply and credit contracts. The authors argue that this is because the break with an international monetary standard produced an upheaval in the processes whereby interest rates, exchange rates, and raw material prices are formed, and hence in the expectations of the sellers, while also exacerbating the insecurity of the buyers about the stability of the contracts concluded.[52]

Since stable contracts are not feasible, producers are obliged to establish their prices bearing in mind the expectation of an unforeseeable evolution of prices. Tavares and Belluzzo suggest that in view of this fact, we now have a system of flexible prices:

> Uncertainty about the user cost of stocks of raw materials and about the current value of past debt are the two decisive elements for conversion of the fixflex price model into a flexible prices model.

In my view this latter proposition is debatable. However much pricing decisions are subject to review, the pricing process is still characterized by a rigidity that derives from the existence of time lags between the moment a pricing decision is made and the time at which effective costs are determined. Even when there is uncertainty about the evolution of costs, pricing decisions are decisions about "regulated prices" (prices which are fixed or adjustable according to some explicit rule) established in contracts and set for a given period, however short. So the decisions in question involve expectations and entail risk.

For a clearer idea of the implications of this fact, it may be worthwhile recalling the argument put forward by Frenkel (1979), even though it was confined to the analysis of an episodic situation involving inflationary shocks determined exogenously and randomly. Frenkel argued that markups remain stable only if the agents who decide prices expect costs to go on rising at the same pace as in the preceding period. If, however, the expectation is that costs will rise at a faster pace, markups will be "inflated" by this increment. As Frenkel shows, the fact that production takes time introduces an element which complicates the determination of markups in inflationary environments. In such environments, the markup has two components: one is related to the desired profit margin which assures a real return on capital, and the other to the expectation of a nominal rise in costs. When this second component tends to accelerate for some reason, that is, when costs are expected to rise faster, markups increase preventively as a way of avoiding an *ex post* profit squeeze. Thus, if the economy is hit by an inflationary shock, production agents in all sectors expect increased variation in their costs, and as a result they endeavor to increase their markups preventively. The size of the increase poses a problem: if they underestimate, they will lose because their margins will after all be squeezed; if they overestimate, they will lose because they sell less. So the choice is a risky one. Frenkel shows that a rational decision-making process leads eventually to a predilection to avoid the error of understanding cost rises. When inflationary shocks occur, an element of acceleration appears because of the bias of overestimating expected cost rises.[53]

It is worth examining the implications of Frenkel's argument in the context of the more general and more relevant propositions developed by Tavares and Belluzzo. Following the breakdown of the international monetary standard, the expectation that significant variations in costs would repeatedly occur meant that the behavior Frenkel described as circumscribed to episodic shock situations in fact became a general rule. It is therefore quite unrealistic to use the notion of normality in pricing, although the more general theoretical conception of two price systems (fix and flex) remains valid, contrary to the argument presented by Tavares and Belluzzo. The difference now is that desired markups are reviewed in each new period, and always incorporate an additional protective margin—the more unstable the economy, the bigger the margin.

In short, the idea of price normality can be sustained only as a simplifying hypothesis about the pricing process under conditions of stability. In an economy with chronic inflation and subject to an endless succession of shocks and adjustment policies, not to mention an international context in which parameters no longer exist for the establishment of normal "prices" for foreign exchange, interest, and raw materials, no analysis that uses a fixed markup rule can hold water.

To conclude, these remarks were intended to show the need for a theory capable of dealing with the mechanisms which, in conditions of acute instability, tend to lead desired markups to play the role of a fundamental price accelerator. (This does not eliminate the possibility of accelerations caused by exogenous shocks.) To develop such a theory, it is necessary to rethink the process by which prices and desired markups are formed. I believe that prices are neither a mechanism for adjusting demand to supply nor a mechanism for adjusting current cost flows to current revenue flows; rather, they are a crucial variable in the process of capital accumulation. This is not to say that prices are determined in such a way as to produce unlimited accumulation, but simply that the pricing process on the one hand can under no conditions represent a process of decapitalization; and on the other it must act as an alternative means of financing the expansion of capital. Thus, it is necessary to rethink the pricing process as one moment of the more general process of capital accumulation. We need to construct a theoretical mediation that will enable us to analyze pricing in relation to the logic of capital accumulation. In a context of acute instability, the process imposes determinations on pricing which a simple fixed markup rule cannot represent.

4

A THEORETICAL FRAMEWORK FOR ANALYZING SHORT-RUN VARIATIONS IN DESIRED MARKUPS

4.1 Introduction

Given the ideas expounded so far, from the theoretical standpoint, it is now necessary to rethink the pricing process in capitalist economies in such a way as to formulate a representation of this process which is satisfactorily general, i.e., independent of the specific characteristics created by an occasional situation of low instability. These special characteristics are implicit in the particular representation synthesized in the rule of a fixed markup over direct costs.

My starting-point is elementary. The dynamics of prices cannot be explained either by the Walrasian logic of an optimizing rationalization of exchanges of a given output, or by the immediate logic of a dispute among sectors and classes for a given income.[1] The pricing process is first and foremost a dimension of capital accumulation, and it is on the basis of the essential aspects of this dynamic that the processes of pricing and formation of desired markups must be theoretically construed.[2]

Like production levels, prices and desired markups are decided in view of the oligopolies' expansion strategy.[3] Investment decisions are interconnected with decisions on pricing and production programming. However, as Minsky points out, you cannot plan for investment without planning for its financing.[4] This means that processes of decision making about prices, desired markups, production volumes, investments, and financing schemes are not isolated; on the contrary, they constitute several dimensions of a single process whereby individual capitalists define their accumulation strategy.

In addition to not being isolated, the determination of prices and markups, as particular dimensions of the determination of the dynamics of individual capital accumulation, takes place on the basis of given structures. The strategic arbitration of individual capital units is conducted in view of the existence of the other capital units. Thus, through market structures, competition establishes the space within which particular price decisions can occur. This structural determination of desired markups, as Possas shows (1985), in the last instance reflects the barriers against entry to each industry. Their variations correspond to changes in the structural nature of industries and of the economy.[5]

Last but not least, it must be stressed that markups and prices are determined in a context of uncertainty. The temporal dimension of capitalist production makes the pricing process speculative in nature because of the uncertainty about the evolution of price-cost ratios over time. Hence decisions on production and prices are also decisions on the use of capital about whose future value there is uncertainty. When they establish protective margins against potential capital losses resulting from the use of capital—margins conditioned by the structural positions of firms—such decisions are also speculative, which means that prices and markups are affected by expectations. In a context of intense uncertainty, expectations tend to play a predominant role in the pricing process, as will be seen below.

In this chapter I develop a theoretical framework for the study of short-run variations in desired markups. To do so I propose a theoretical synthesis between the strategic and the expectational determinations of markups and prices, given a set of market structures. The chapter is divided into four sections. Following this introduction there is a synthesis of the main arguments presented by post-Keynesians on what I have termed the strategic determination of desired markups. I then reclaim Keynes's concept of user cost, which in my opinion captures well the expectational determination of desired markups. Finally I propose an analytical integration of these two determinations, given a set of market and economic structures. This integration is summarized in a general formula for desired markups.

4.2 The New Microeconomics and the Strategic Dimension of Desired Markups

The non-conventional literature on microeconomics has developed a series of important contributions to the formulation of a theoretical framework as an alternative to the static-marginalist analysis of the firm and industry which is characteristic of conventional thinking.[6]

According to Eichner (1985), these contributions already comprise a body of theory that can be substituted for neoclassical analysis and could be called the "new microeconomics."

> Economists have long been aware that the orthodox microeconomic theory has little relevance to the contemporary situation. What they generally do not realize is that there now exists an alternative body of theory—one which, though no less comprehensive and no less coherent, corresponds far more closely to what can be observed in the real world of corporate enterprise. This alternative body of theory, which represents a synthesis of certain ideas to be found within the managerial,[7] behavioralist,[8] institutionalist,[9] and post-Keynesian literature,[10] can be termed the new microeconomics. (Eichner 1985, 28)

In a previous work he had already presented a synthetic formulation of the "new microeconomics" critique of the orthodox view of price determination under oligopoly.

> For an understanding of how prices are determined under oligopoly it is necessary to examine, not the conditions affecting the individual firm in the short run, but rather the conditions affecting the industry as a whole over the long run. This extension of the analysis to multiple periods not only introduces time as a factor, it also means that the pricing decision cannot be divorced from the industry's investment planning. (Eichner 1976, 55)

Eichner (1973; 1976; 1985) formulated a model which is representative of the "new microeconomics" on the subject of pricing. The model provides an overall framework that synthesizes the main contributions made by this alternative microeconomic literature—by now a vast body of work—particularly with regard to what I have denominated the strategic determination of desired markups. This model also helps to integrate the notion of user cost, so as to establish a theoretical framework capable of analyzing the short-run behavior of desired markups.

As in his earlier work, Eichner (1985) starts with the idea that in contemporary capitalism pricing decisions are related and subordinated to oligopolies' expansion strategy.[11] In a study written in 1976 (chap. 2), he described the nature of the "megacorp," which in his view had the following distinctive features: (a) management and ownership of the firm are separate; (b) it operates multiple plants with fixed factors; (c) it takes part in at least one oligopolized industry. In the same chapter he defines oligopoly and shows that in spite of anti-trust laws there are mechanisms for coordination of firms in oligopolies which prevent the occurrence of competition through price wars. On the contrary, firms tend to coordinate decisions through a system of price leadership in which the leading firm (usually but not necessarily the biggest) determines the price which will prevail in the short run. This firm therefore acts as representative of the industry insofar as it endeavors to establish prices to the advantage of the whole industry with a view to maximum growth as well as the stability of its industrial structure:

> While the laws of the United States prohibit the members of any industry from conferring together over prices, various informal channels of communication nonetheless exist. Interviews granted to trade magazines, statements made at stockholder meetings, and similar public utterances by megacorp officials serve to create an industrywide consensus that the price leader must necessarily take into account before making its pricing decision. This is not to deny that the actual price decided upon is likely to be calculated to advance the price leader's own interests or that the other members of the industry, if the decision were theirs to make, might choose some other figure. But—and this is the premise on which the analysis that follows will be based—the price leader in deciding upon a particular price is in effect acting on behalf of the entire industry. (Eichner 1976, 42)[12]

Thus the practice of price leadership and the possibility of using the idea that the leader's decisions are representative of the industry's decisions derive from the structural nature of the market in which collective destruction is to be avoided:

> To speak of the industry in this connection is, of course, to speak of the megacorp-price leader. Its practice of acting as the surrogate for its fellow oligopolists arises out of a real necessity—the need of an industry to avoid price competition that will be destructive to all its members. (Eichner 1976, 55)

Through his model Eichner argues that the pricing process is subordinated to the logic of deciding how to fund a set of investments seen as strategic for the expansion of the oligopolies. Eichner's synthesis of this process can be seen in figure 9, where the desired variation of profit margins over average production costs (*mb*, lower lefthand quadrant) is determined from the quantity and makeup of the funds required for the additional investment which will optimize the leader's long-term position. The total amount of funding (Fc) is made up of an internal portion (Fb) and a portion of external origin ($Fc - Fb$): "It (the price) is determined based on the price previously prevailing in the industry and the change in that price necessary to provide the megacorp-price leader with the additional investment funds[13] needed to optimize its long-run market position—provided that the implicit interest charge on those additional internal funds is not greater than the cost of external funds" (Eichner 1976, 101).

The increased margins over average production costs allow for the possibility of expanding the net amount of funds to the firm. But according to Eichner there are three types of costs implicit in this alternative: (a) the substitution effect, which in practice represents the implicit cost of the additional internal funds obtained in the initial periods resulting from the drop in the growth of sales in the industry over time;[14] (b) the entry factor, i.e., the implicit cost in the decline in sales resulting from the possible entry of new firms made feasible by the increase in profit margins;[15] (c) the possible resulting government retaliations.[16]

In Eichner's model these three implicit costs can be aggregated and synthesized in the R curve of the upper lefthand quadrant in figure. 9.[17] The R curve shows not only that the implicit cost (R) associated with different alternatives for

Figure 9

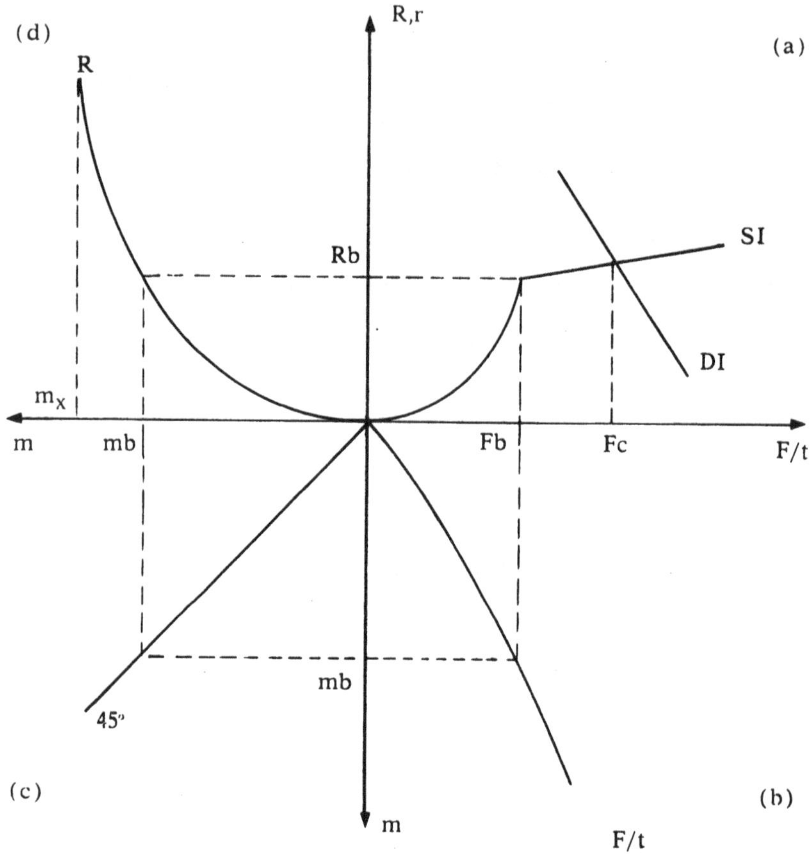

markup increases (mb)[18] is ascending but also that R rises at increasing rates and tends towards a level after which it will no longer be possible to go on increasing markups, since the implicit cost beyond this limit would be infinite. This is because such increases would be correlated with probabilities the megacorp could not accept as regards the risk of entry to the market by new firms[19] or of government intervention:

> If n [changed here to m] continues to rise still higher, the megacorp-price leader will finally encounter the ceiling imposed by the maximum acceptable probability of either new entry or meaningful government intervention. This ceiling, n_x [here m_x as in fig. 9], is the percentage increase in price for which either the associated q (probability of new firm entry) exceeds $X1$ (acceptable maximum for this probability) or the associated p (probability of government retaliation) exceeds $X2$ (acceptable maximum for this probability), depending on which upper limit is encountered first. Once n_x has been reached, the value of R will, insofar as the megacorp-price leader is concerned, become infinitely large. (Eichner 1976, 83-84)[20]

Although such increases in margins represent costs, they also make additional funds available for investment. This relationship between increases in margins and increases in the availability of net funds for additional investments is expressed in the lower right-hand quadrant of figure 9. Because of the substitution and entry effects, funds for investment increase at a falling rate in relation to the increase of markups.[21] Eichner combines this curve with the curve relating implicit costs to increases in margins, and the result is a curve for the supply of internal funds for investment (marked SI' in figure 10).

However, there is an alternative possibility; funds can be obtained by issuing new credit instruments or shares to the public. The cost of these can be represented by a positively inclined straight line (fig.10), indicating costs of funds (r) which increase in relation to their volume.[22]

When it decides to proceed with a given instrument, a firm endeavors to fund the amount so as to minimize its costs, and this action is synthesized in curve SI (fig. 10), which assumes

Figure 10

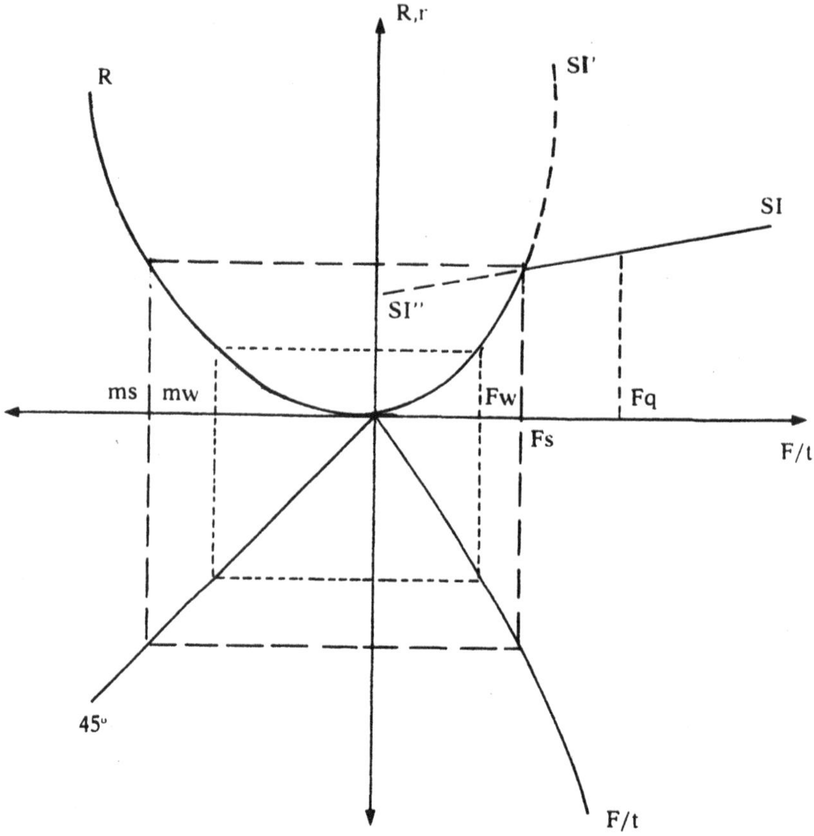

the lowest value between the two curves representing the implicit costs associated with the raising of the internal funds (SI') and external funds (SI''). According to the corresponding curve in figure 10, this means the following: for any amount of required additional funds, Fw, where $Fw < Fs$ all financing will be done by means of internal funds and the increase will be equal to mw, as shown in the figure. For any amount of required funds equal to Fq, where $Fq > Fs$, the firm will increase its markup by ms and will borrow externally the amount equivalent to $Fq - Fs$.

It remains to be seen how the volume of funds required for additional investment is to be determined. Eichner suggests that in accordance with its expansion strategy the leading firm has a set of investment projects which are linked to its maximum long-run expansion goal and with which different rates of return on investment are associated.

> Assuming for the moment that technological change is entirely capital embodied[23] a megacorp-price leader interested in but a single industry will be faced with a choice among four types of investment expenditures, each of which can be expected to affect the growth of the corporate levy in the long run and each of which will thus have its own marginal efficiency of investment schedule. These four types of investment expenditures can be categorized as follows: (a) the purchase of new plant and equipment, (b) the differentiation of the industry's product more sharply, (c) the erection of higher barriers to entry, or (d) the creation of more favorable public image.[24] The varying additional amounts of F/t that can be spent on each of the four categories at varying prospective rates of return, r, is what defines the megacorp-price leader's overall marginal efficiency of investment schedule. This overall MEI schedule, in turn, is what constitutes the megacorp leader's total demand curve of investment funds, DI. (Eichner 1976, 88–89)

The comparison between this investment fund demand curve and the overall curve of investment fund availability (which equals the minimum cost between external and internal funds—curve SI) determines the level of additional investment, which in figure 9 represents the point of intersection between curves DI and SI.

Thus the investments decided upon as a result of the oligopolies' expansion strategies and the definition of their funding pattern determine the strategic increase of markups, given certain external costs and the likelihood of new firm entry, government intervention, and the risks associated with the substitution effect.

4.3 The Concept of User Cost in Keynes and the Expectational Dimension of Desired Markups

The concept of user cost, having been briefly touched upon at the start of chapter 3 of *The General Theory*, is introduced at the start of chapter 6 when Keynes points out that in order to arrive at a concept of income in the current period it is necessary to account for a flow due to the equipment inherited from the previous period (Keynes 1965, 53). In my opinion this concept is one of the links in the theoretical mediation to be constructed between the logic of capital accumulation and price determination in capitalist economies, as I endeavor to show in what follows.

One of Keynes's main contributions in *The General Theory* (1965) was his study of the basic aspects of capitalist decisions, i.e., the study of the elements which determine capitalist calculation. The concept of user cost is part of this approach. It is a key element of calculation for short-run decisions, regarding the definition of prices and level of utilization of a "capital equipment" resulting from investment and production decisions taken in the past.[25]

The hub of the matter for Keynes is that the determination of prices and of the level of current production depends on a prospective, subjective, and specific calculation by each decision-making unit, regarding the "user cost of capital" (depreciation of the capital stock or loss of capital value in the sense of transfer of its value to the product) implicit in the realization of a certain level of production.[26] This "capital loss" is different from others that may occur during the production period because of its deliberate nature. It is a "capital loss" which results from the decision to realize a given level of production.[27]

User cost is calculated with reference to the expected lifetime of the existing "capital equipment." This is the basic meaning of Keynes's remark that user cost is "one of the links between the present and the future."

Keynes situates himself in the Marshallian tradition of price determination. For him, prices are determined in the short run on the basis of costs and of the principle of profit maximization, whereby marginal revenue equals marginal prime cost. But one basic point where he differs from Marshall is that for Keynes prime cost is not confined to factor cost:

> Now in the modern theory of value it has been a usual practice to equate the short-period supply price to the marginal factor cost alone. It is obvious, however, that this is only legitimate if marginal user cost is zero or if supply price is specially defined. . . . But, whereas it may occasionally be convenient in dealing with *output as a whole* to deduct user cost, this procedure deprives our analysis of all reality if it is habitually (and tacitly) applied to the output of a single industry or firm, since it divorces the 'supply price' of an article from any ordinary sense of its 'price'; and some confusion may have resulted from the practice of doing so. (Keynes 1965, 67)

For Keynes, then, there is an additional element in prime cost—the user cost of existing capital equipment associated with a certain level of production.

For Keynes, what determines the amount of user cost is "the expected sacrifice of future benefit involved in present use" of capital equipment (Keynes 1965, 70). Here he defines user cost as "the reduction in the value of the equipment due to using it as compared with not using it, after allowing for the cost of the maintenance and improvements which it would be worth while to undertake and for purchase from other entrepreneurs" (ibid.).

User cost can be perceived by the difference in value of a given stock of capital in two hypothetical situations: that of not producing, which would leave the remaining capital equipment with a value equal to $G' - B'$ where G' corresponds to the value of the existing capital equipment if nothing is produced and B' is the cost of maintaining the capital equipment; and that of realizing production such that a capital loss equal to $U(A)$ would result (the user cost associated with a level of production A), leaving a remaining capital value equal to $G - A1$. G is in fact the remaining capital equipment—to obtain the user cost it is also necessary to subtract $A1$, corresponding to purchases from other capitalists during the production period. In other words, user cost $U(A)$ is equal to the difference between $(G' - B')$ and $(G - A1)$.

Therefore, what is in question is a difference between capitals, whose magnitudes are determined by the prospective calculations of entrepreneurs as to future evolution of the values corresponding to replacement cost, supplementary cost, and maintenance cost for "capital equipment."

Thus a capitalist will reduce the prospective value of his capital only if his current production is realized at a price that can guarantee coverage of all costs, including the cost associated with expected capital loss, as well as providing an adequate return on capital. The prospects of capital appreciation in the future are brought forward into the present, simultaneously determining the levels of production and prices, by means of calculating the user cost, which in this way becomes a "link between the present and the future."

How does a capitalist speculatively reckon the user cost associated with a given level of production? According to Keynes, "it must be arrived at . . . by calculating the discounted value of the additional prospective yield which would be obtained at some later date if it [the equipment] were not used now . . . Today's user cost is equal to the maximum of the discounted values of the potential expected yields of all the tomorrows" (Keynes 1965, 70 and note 1).

Consequently the user cost associated with a given production is the maximum of the values expected from the capital which is about to be used during the remaining life of the capital equipment, discounted at rates which are subjective and specific to each productive agent, and taking into account the relative supplementary and maintenance costs in case there is a delay in using the capital equipment.[28]

By highlighting the fundamental role of expectations in capitalists' calculations and short-run decisions, therefore,

Keynes brought into the open the speculative nature of the pricing process under capitalist conditions.[29] For Keynes, prices do not reflect a mere interplay of relations established at a given moment, for they have dynamic determinations which invalidate analyses limited to static determinations.[30] Prices also reflect capitalists' subjective and specific assessments of the conditions for capital equipment to appreciate and grow during the expected remaining life of the capital. Thus expectations about the future are one of the factors that determine current prices.

It is my contention, therefore, that when Keynes formulated the concept of user cost he laid the groundwork for an analysis of the expectational dimension of prices and desired markups. Keynes's specific formulation regarding short-run prices, following the marginalist principles whereby marginal revenue equals marginal prime cost, should not obscure the more general principles exposed above. For this reason, the notion of user cost is a necessary component, implicitly or explicitly, in any explanation of the price formation process in capitalist economies, given that pricing decisions are subordinated to the capital accumulation process and that capitalist decisions are taken under conditions of uncertainty. The concept of user cost makes it possible to establish one of the links in the theoretical mediation between price determination and capital accumulation.

For this reason employing the concept of user cost in explanations of the pricing process is not only valid in all situations (low and high instability) but is necessary to all general theoretical formulations on the pricing process. However, in conditions of relatively low instability, that is, when economic events are reasonably foreseeable for a relevant period of time, the rule of a fixed markup may be a simple and adequate way of defining prices, given that sharp changes in the value of the components of capital equipment or in demand levels are unlikely. Both prices and demand are likely to fluctuate "normally" around levels that permit a match between reproduction of the market structure and an "expected rate" of capital accumulation through a simple markup rule. In other words, under conditions of low instability in capitalist economies, the rule of fixed markup may adequately represent the pricing process, without explicitly bringing user cost into the analysis. In a context of pronounced instability, however, user cost must be the object of explicit analysis. With this goal in mind, in what follows I develop a formal treatment of the concept of user cost in such a way as to integrate it with the other factors determining prices and desired markups.

In accordance with the above exposition, user cost is equal to the present value of the greatest expected value of that part of capital used in production, taking as a temporal reference for the comparison between expected values the period during which the capital equipment will remain useable and employing discount rates specific to each one of the moments and to each capitalist, as well as specific rates for supplementary and maintenance costs.

If we have a capital equipment A with a value A^*, its user cost will have a value corresponding to the use fraction a, directly related to the level of its physical use, multiplied by its value and by a factor equal to the maximum expected appreciation, discounted at a specific interest rate, taking into consideration the supplementary and maintenance costs incurred if the capital equipment were not used. Thus:

$$U(A) = \max[a \cdot A^*(1+v_t)^t(1-s_t)^t(1-m_t)^t/(1+r_t)^t] \quad (1)$$

$$v_t = (p_t/p_0)^{1/t} - 1 \quad (2)$$

for $t = 1, 2 \ldots n$ and $V_0 = 0$;
where:

- $U(A)$ is the user cost of A;
- v_t is the rate of appreciation expected for A in a period of time t;
- r_t is the average interest rate expected for a set of periods $1 \ldots t$;
- s_t is the rate of the supplementary cost over a period t;
- m_t is the rate of the maintenance cost over a period t;
- n is the remaining period in the working life of capital equipment A;
- p_t is the expected value of the good corresponding to A;[31]
- p_0 is the value of the good corresponding to A.

By bringing to the fore the product $a \cdot A^*$, expression (1) can be rewritten as follows:

$$U(A) = a \cdot A^* \cdot \max\{[(1 + v_t)(1 - s_t)(1 - m_t)/(1 + r_t)]^t\}. \quad (3)$$

If the values of variables v_t, s_t, m_t, r_t and t corresponding to their maximum points are written with an asterisk (*), we have:

$$U(A) = a \cdot A^*[(1 + v_t^*)(1 - s_t^*)(1 - m_t^*)/(1 + r_t^*)]^{t^*}]. \quad (4)$$

To simplify, we can write this as:

$$\rho^A = [(1 + v_t^*)(1 - s_t^*)(1 - m_t^*)/(1 + r_t^*)]^{t^*} \quad (5)$$

where:

> ρ^A is the maximum index of appreciation expected for the good corresponding to capital A, or the user cost index of A.

Thus if we substitute (5) in (4), user cost can be expressed:

$$U(A) = a \cdot A^* \cdot \rho^A. \quad (6)$$

Another way of expressing the user cost of A, $U(A)$, can be derived by substituting the term $a \cdot A^*$, which represents the used part of capital A at current prices, with a term which makes explicit the product of used amounts of A and their individual prices. Thus, if:

$$a \cdot A^* = p^A \cdot q^A \quad (7)$$

and if this is substituted in (6), we have:

$$U(A) = p^A \cdot q^A \cdot \rho^A \quad (8)$$

where:

> p^A is the current price of the good A;
> q^A is the amount of A actually used.

Now let us see how these ideas can be used to work out the determinants of changes in desired markups.

4.4 A General Formulation for Desired Markups for the Purpose of Analyzing Their Short-Run Variations

My objective here is to arrive at a general formulation for desired markups which can permit analysis of their variations in the short run and account for the three dimensions of markups—structural, strategic, and expectational. To achieve this objective, it is best to start with the simplest and most general identity a firm administering its prices can have as a basic reference point for planning: that is, that the expected revenue must be equal to the total expected costs plus the gross profits required if the firm's strategic goals are to be met, bearing in mind the various constraints it faces:

$$R = C + L \tag{9}$$

where:

R is the expected revenue;
C is the total expected costs;
L is the gross profit required to meet the firm's strategic goals.

Costs can in turn be divided into two types: $C(X)$, costs which depend on the level of production X; and $C(K)$, costs which depend on the size of capital. Thus expression (9) can be rewritten as follows:

$$R = C(X) + C(K) + L. \tag{10}$$

This expression can be broken down by detailing each of its four terms, as shown in expressions (11) through (14) below, followed by explanations of their meanings:

$$R = p \cdot X \tag{11}$$
$$C(X) = w \cdot b \cdot X + p_m \cdot m \cdot \rho_m \cdot X + p_k \cdot d_k \cdot \rho_k \cdot X \tag{12}$$
$$C(K) = d^* \cdot K + j \cdot K \tag{13}$$
$$L = s \cdot K + t \cdot K \tag{14}$$

where:

p is the product price;
x is the expected sales volume;

w is the wage per worker;
b is the inverse of the productivity per worker;
p_m is the current price of raw materials;
m is the coefficient of raw material utilization per unit of output;
ρ_m is the maximum index of expected real appreciation in the value of raw materials;
p_k is the price of the capital good utilized;
d_k is that portion of depreciation per unit of capital which depends on utilization;
ρ_k is the maximum index of expected real appreciation in the value of the capital good;
j is the indirect production cost associated with the size of capital;[32]
d^* is the supplementary cost, i.e., the involuntary but foreseeable capital loss;
K is capital in value terms;
s is the current profit rate;
t is the increment in the current profit rate required for the oligopolies' new strategic decisions to be implemented.[33]

Expression (11) is trivial and self-explanatory. Expected gross revenue equals the product of the expected sales volume times the planned prices. Expression (12) presents the various components of the costs associated with production volume. The first term corresponds to the cost of labor, as in conventional price equations. The second term stands for the cost of raw materials, here modified by multiplication by the user-cost index for the raw materials in question, in accordance with the formula for user cost outlined in the preceding section. In addition to these two terms, expression (12) includes a term for the user cost of capital goods which represents a portion of depreciation. This point requires further explanation.

As we have seen, for Keynes depreciation of capital goods has two components. One depends on the level of utilization, and is thus a voluntary component of depreciation. The other is involuntary and depends not on the level of production but on the size of capital—this is what Keynes calls supplementary cost:

> Now some part of these involuntary (capital) losses, whilst they are unavoidable, are—broadly speaking—not unexpected; such as losses through the lapse of time irrespective of use, and also 'normal' obsolescence which, as Professor Pigou expresses it, "is sufficiently regular to be foreseen, if not in detail, at least in the large," including, we may add, those losses to the community as a whole which are sufficiently regular to be commonly regarded as 'insurable risks'. Let us ignore for the moment the fact that the amount of the expected loss depends on when the expectation is assumed to be framed, and let us call the depreciation of the equipment, which is involuntary but not unexpected, i.e., the excess of the expected depreciation over the user cost, the supplementary cost, which will be written V. (Keynes 1965, 56)

Thus the third term in expression (12) represents that part of depreciation which exceeds supplementary cost and depends on the level of production and on a user-cost index specific to capital goods.

Expression (13) presents the two components of costs which do not depend on production volume and can be expressed directly as proportions of capital.[34] First, we have supplementary cost which, as already stated, corresponds to that part of depreciation which exceeds the user cost of capital equipment and facilities. Secondly, we have the various costs associated with all the firm's obligations which do not change with production volume, ranging from salaries paid to administrative personnel to payments related to financial obligations. The latter item can include payment of dividends, as Eichner noted.[35] Two further remarks regarding the costs that do not depend on production volume are pertinent. First, among the firm's financial commitments we can include the obligations assumed with the aim of forming a financial portfolio that can serve as a hedge against the increase in financial costs associated with the cost of working capital that might occur if interest rates rose. If a financial hedge exists, any such increases in costs will be offset by increase in financial revenue. The costs incurred by these operations are an obligation that does not depend on production volume. Secondly, we can conceivably isolate a third component corresponding to the third type of capital loss (in addition to user cost and supplementary cost), i.e., unforeseen (or "windfall") losses. But this term can be left out if the practice of insurance is borne in mind. On the other hand insurance increases the value of fixed obligations (j), as is the case with the other financial costs which do not depend on production volume.

Finally, expression (14) presents two terms corresponding to total gross profit. The first is current yield in terms of the invested capital, covering all the firm's various kinds of investment (understood in the sense Eichner defines this word) and reflecting the structural determination of markups. The second term is a transformed version of the increment in markups required for internal funding of the additional investments needed for the firm's strategy but that are not fundable by $s \cdot K$.[36]

If we substitute (11), (12), (13), and (14) in (10) we have:

$$p \cdot X = w \cdot b \cdot X + p_m \cdot m \cdot \rho_m \cdot X + p_k \cdot d_k \cdot \rho_k \cdot X + j \cdot K + d^* \cdot K + s \cdot K + t \cdot k. \quad (15)$$

And if we divide by X and proceed with some algebraic manipulations we obtain:

$$p = w \cdot b + p_m \cdot m \cdot \rho_m + p_k \cdot d \cdot \rho_k + (j + d^* + s + t) \cdot K/X. \quad (16)$$

Let:

$$h = j + d^* + s \quad (17)$$

and:

$$k = K/(p \cdot X^*) \quad (18)$$

where:

k is the ratio of capital to output;
x^* is maximum production.

Given that component t of the gross profit is simply an alternative way of expressing the increment in the desired markup according to Eichner's formulation, we have:

$$t \cdot K = m^* \cdot X \cdot (w \cdot b + p_m \cdot m); \tag{19}$$

or:

$$t = m^* \cdot X \cdot (w \cdot b + p_m \cdot m)/K \tag{20}$$

where:

m^* is a function of the additional demand for investment funds required to implement an oligopoly's strategy, as in Eichner's formulation.

If we substitute (17), (18), and (20) in (16), we obtain:

$$p = w \cdot b + p_m \cdot m \cdot \rho_m + p_k \cdot d_k \cdot \rho_k + h \cdot k \cdot p \cdot X^*/X + m^* \cdot (w \cdot b + p_m \cdot m). \tag{21}$$

Since

$$v = X/X^*; \tag{22}$$

where:

v is the level of capacity utilization, we have:[37]

$$p \cdot (1 - h \cdot k/v) = w \cdot b + p_m \cdot m \cdot \rho_m + p_k \cdot d_k \cdot \rho_k + m^* \cdot (w \cdot b + p_m \cdot m). \tag{23}$$

Since our aim is to analyze the determinants of changes in desired markups over the costs of labor and raw materials, let:

$$p = (1 + z)(w \cdot b + p_m \cdot m) \tag{24}$$

where:

z is the desired markup.

If we substitute p as defined in (24) in (23), we have:

$$(1 + z)(w \cdot b + p_m \cdot m)(1 - h \cdot k/v) = w \cdot b + p_m \cdot m \cdot \rho_m + p_k \cdot d_k \cdot \rho_k + m^*(w \cdot b + p_m \cdot m). \tag{25}$$

An algebraic reworking of this expression produces the following:

$$z = (w \cdot b + p_m \cdot m \cdot \rho_m)/[(w \cdot b + p_m \cdot m)(1 - h \cdot k/v)] + (p_k \cdot d_k \cdot \rho_k)/[w \cdot b + p_m \cdot m)(1 - h \cdot k/v)] + m^*/(1 - h \cdot k/v) - 1. \qquad (26)$$

By letting:

$$c = w \cdot b + p_m \cdot m \qquad (27)$$

$$f = w \cdot b/c \qquad (28)$$

$$y = p_k \cdot d_k/c \qquad (29)$$

where:

c is the unit cost of labor and raw materials at current prices;
f is labor cost as a proportion of c;[38]
y is the ratio of fixed capital cost to labor and raw material costs;[39] and by introducing (27), (28), and (29) into (26) with some simplification, we have:

$$z = [c \cdot f + c \cdot (1 - f) \cdot \rho_m]/[c \cdot (1 - h \cdot k/v)] + y \cdot \rho_k/(1 - h \cdot k/v) + m^*/(1 - h \cdot k/v) - 1 \qquad (30)$$

which can be transformed into a synthetic formulation of desired markups:

$$z = [f + (1 - f) \cdot \rho_m + y \cdot \rho_k + m^*]/(1 - h \cdot k/v) - 1. \qquad (31)$$

This is a general expression for desired markups. It is not very hard to see from this formula the factors that determine short-run variations in markups, whether in an upward or downward direction.[40] My next step, in chapter 5, will be to transform this general expression into a particular form suitable for studying the short-run behavior of desired markups in the context of an economy under adjustment.

5

ADJUSTMENT, INFLATION, AND THE SHORT-RUN BEHAVIOR OF DESIRED MARKUPS: INTRODUCTORY NOTES

As already observed, the study of inflationary processes using analytical structures which include the hypothesis of a fixed markup can be conducted only under specific circumstances in a capitalist economy, i.e., under conditions of low instability. For this reason, and given my aim of studying the characteristics of inflationary processes in economies under adjustment, in chapter 4 I performed the preliminary task of constructing a general theoretical framework for the analysis of short-run variations in desired markups.[1]

Hence the schema outlined above provides a basis for examining the dynamic behavior of prices under oligopoly. It establishes general principles for analyzing the dynamics of inflation in economies dominated by oligopolies.[2] However, as I stressed at the beginning of this book, inflationary processes must be understood as historically determined processes.[3] Thus, to understand the characteristics of such a process it is necessary to specify a particular formula for analysis, using as a starting-point the general formula presented in the preceding chapter.

My endeavor at this stage is specifically to study some particular characteristics which have emerged as part of inflationary processes[4] in economies under the following conditions, some of which are mutually correlated:[5]

(a) a significantly complex productive structure—that is, a diversified economy with a high degree of integration, with significant inter-industry relations, and with oligopolies holding hegemony in processes of decision making on production, investment, and prices ("corporate economy");[6]

(b) chronic inflation;[7]

(c) the state plays a major role in the pricing process because it produces intermediate goods consumed by several industries, supplies items with considerable weight in the formation of several prices, and defines the structure and weight of the taxes which impinge on the costs and final prices of a number of products;

(d) the financial position of the public sector is fragile, in the sense to be defined below;

(e) the economy is undergoing an adjustment process.[8]

As a first step, I begin with a general characterization of the impacts of adjustment processes, especially as regards the variables that affect the dynamics of inflation. A particular expression of the formula on desired markups developed in the preceding chapter then follows. This is designed to apply to the study of inflationary dynamics in countries with the above-mentioned characteristics. The central point is that the economic adjustment forced upon the debtor nations in recent years has caused: (a) major uncertainties with regard to the future prices of producer goods (raw materials and capital goods) which are imported and/or intensely used to produce exportable goods; and (b) financial fragility in the public sector. This fragility has in some cases become so serious that it has finally led to inflationary pressures deriving to a large degree from the rise in the user cost of public-fiscal goods.[9]

To clarify these points I briefly introduce the relations between adjustment and inflation, then give general characterization of adjustment processes and examine their general impacts, highlighting the changes caused in the liabilities of the public sector. The main indirect inflationary impacts of adjustment processes are then pointed out.[10] Finally I present the particular formulation of desired markups appropriate to the study of price dynamics under adjustment.

5.1 Adjustment and Inflation: Preliminary Remarks

The dynamics of inflation in economies undergoing adjustment are closely related to the characteristics of the adjustment processes. What is the nature of this relation, in general terms? The main instruments used in adjustment efforts have been exchange, fiscal, and monetary policies. In addition to acting directly upon the process of price formation and accelerating inflation, these policies strongly accentuate the growing financial fragility of the public sector. This, together with expectations of recurrent changes in interest and exchange rates, radically alters the dynamics of prices, leading desired markups to play an active role in the acceleration of inflation.

It is worth examining in more detail how each of these parts relates to the others. I first show how the process of adjustment has affected the economies in question, both in general and at the level of the main instruments of economic policy. I then specify what I mean by financial fragility of the public sector, a concept which differs from that of public-sector deficit. The next step will be to give a general idea of how the financial fragility of the public sector and expectations of changes in interest and exchange rates can affect the pricing mechanism.

5.2 Adjustment and Its Effects on Expectations about Economic Policy and the Liabilities of the Public Sector

The first key aspects to be analyzed here are the general and external impacts of adjustment. In the late 1970s the U.S. government forced all the heavily indebted nations to undergo drastic adjustment as a "side effect" of its own economic policy.[11] Rising international interest rates in the late 1970s led to a complex series of movements with highly perverse effects on the economies which had become significantly indebted in the preceding period.[12] Initially the increase in interest rates aggravated the foreign currency problems faced by the debtor nations, as the cost of debt service soared while the sources of foreign currency earnings remained constant. This instability on the exchange front stimulated speculation against the local currency in these countries. Given the deterioration in the country's balance of payments caused by the increased cost of indebtedness, the private sector sought to conduct all its operations under the assumption that exchange policy would continue to suffer discontinuity. In view of this prospect, the private sector endeavored to avoid taking out new foreign loans, passed on to the public sector the loans it had made in the past, and transformed most of its funds and contracts into foreign currency in order to cut losses and even obtain advantages should its expectations of sharp devaluations in the exchange rate be confirmed. These movements both caused greater difficulties with foreign exchange, thereby aggravating the processes themselves, and created more complex problems in managing the situation, given the private sector's unwillingness to take new foreign loans.

Among the economic policy reactions to this situation were both the elevation of domestic interest rates and a series of major devaluations of the local currency against the dollar. Both of these factors aggravated still further the difficulty of managing the foreign debt in countries under adjustment. Increases in internal interest rates in an effort to stimulate the entry of foreign loans and to minimize capital flight aggravated the domestic economic crisis, which restricted even more the overall demand for credit, making the process of recycling external debts more and more dependent on direct state action. The state, in turn, not only rapidly took on a growing share in the foreign debt but was obliged to shoulder most of the burden of policies increasing exchange and interest rates. The overall outcome of this process was a significant increase in internal interest rates and a progressive deterioration in the financial situation of the public sector, since the latter was forced to become very internally indebted in order to fulfil its swelling commitments to foreign debt service.

In this fashion, the prospects for continued and sustainable economic growth at significant rates were increasingly undermined, which made productive investment less and less attractive. The deterioration in the economic conditions in these countries, exacerbated by the effects of indebtedness on the government's ability to conduct economic policy in an orderly and suitable fashion, fueled the tendency to keep funds on the money market and other financial circuits protected from fluctuations in the exchange rate. Moreover, funds could be very profitably invested on the foreign financial market at appreciable interest rates.

The rise in international interest rates thus attracted funds in two ways: through the high rate of return offered abroad, and through the aggravation in the domestic crisis caused by adjustment policies, leading to capital flight. The immediate outcome of this general and external process of adjustment was a rapid growth in government debt, initially to foreign creditors and then domestically, and exhaustion of the operational effectiveness of the main instruments of economic policy, as will be seen below.

5.3 The Inflationary Impacts of Adjustment Processes: Introductory Remarks

Before beginning a more specific analysis of the relationship between adjustment and inflation, it is important to highlight the fact that adjustment processes cause both direct and indirect inflationary impacts.

The direct impacts are those generally studied by authors analyzing the relations between external adjustment and inflation. They are important and must obviously be considered when the problem is examined in depth. Among these are, for example, the immediate effects of devaluation of the national currency and its impact on the cost of imported raw materials. Along the same lines are the impacts of increases in public-sector charges and prices, increased taxes, and the direct impacts of rises in interest rates insofar as these are financial costs.[13]

The indirect or induced impacts are as important as the direct impacts, if not more so. They result from the effects of adjustment on the determination of desired markups. The increase in interest rates, uncertainty about exchange rates, and the impact of these measures on the government's financial fragility lead firms to establish their desired markups in a different manner from the one which is characteristic during periods of low instability. This tends to cause a succession of inflationary shocks.

I move on now to a more detailed scrutiny of the inflationary impacts caused by adjustment processes. From the standpoint of external adjustment, there tends to be pressure on the inflation process because of the need for abrupt creation of high trade surpluses and their prolonged maintenance. This pressure means, among other possibilities, that the supply of some products on the domestic market will become insufficient in the future, so that speculation with stockpiles of such products becomes more attractive. The need to increase the trade surplus tends to push up future prices for certain products, which in turn leads to an increase in the user cost of these products, and hence to an increase in the prices of the products for which they are used as inputs. Furthermore, external adjustments tend to be inflationary because of the exchange-rate policies which normally accompany them. In addition to the effects of major devaluations, as long as the foreign currency bottleneck persists, the economy remains vulnerable to speculation with the exchange rate by importers of inputs and producers of goods intensively used in the production of exportable goods, and this speculation in turn raises the user cost of these goods.

From the standpoint of internal adjustment, pressures arise from both fiscal and monetary policy. In the case of fiscal policy, the need to cut subsidies and increase taxes and public-sector charges—aimed at reducing the public deficit as a means to contain demand—affects the prices and pricing policies of firms operating at any important point in the network of economic relations through which public-fiscal goods pass.[14] Measures taken to reduce the public deficit not only directly affect prices but eventually, through the expectations which precede such measures, fuel speculation with public-fiscal goods and hence raise the desired markups of firms which use such goods, as a means of offsetting their increased user cost.

As to monetary policy, governments have taken steps to raise domestic interest rates for a number of reasons. Under voluntary adjustment, and while the flow of international credit was maintained, increases in the domestic interest rate were designed to enhance the attractiveness of foreign loans despite uncertainty about exchange rates. Once the flow of external credit had been cut off, increased interest rates were aimed at minimizing capital flight and containing domestic demand. The policy of keeping domestic interest rates high had varying effects on the upward trend of prices. The outstanding effect was aggravation of the financial fragility of the public sector because of a sharp rise in government indebtedness. Public-sector financial fragility in turn tends to generate inflation, both for the reasons already mentioned and because of the factors set out below in a preliminary manner, followed in chapter 6 by a model for analyzing the interactions between inflation and public-sector financial fragility in detail.

Before turning specifically to the relations between these two processes, however, I must clarify what I mean by public-sector financial fragility. As used here, financial fragility does not mean the existence of a public deficit. Strictly speaking, no macroeconomic problems are caused by the existence of a government deficit, be it fiscal or budgetary, as long as it can be financed in an appropriate manner. A deficit can be financed appropriately when there are sources of financing available, and when the cost of financing it does not entail a future inability to go on financing or a very high future cost of financing. Public finances can be kept sound and healthy only when the indebtedness which normally accompanies a deficit occurs at a pace compatible with the normal (i.e., without changes in prices) generation of funds by the public sector and/or with the expansion of its external sources of financing. A situation where there is a deficit and difficulties with financing the deficit—by definition one of fragility—leads to expectations of rising interest rates, given the government's lack of bargaining power with creditors. As a result, when the financial situation of the public sector is fragile, inflation tends to be propelled faster because of uncertainty about the future cost of public-fiscal goods and the future evolution of taxes and subsidies, and their repercussions on the main economic variables. Public-sector financial fragility accelerates uncertainty, above all through increases in the user cost of public-fiscal goods. These then are the basic relations between the financial fragility of the public sector and inflation which will be analyzed in greater detail and formalized in the following chapter.

5.4 An Appropriate Formulation for the Study of the Short-Run Dynamics of Desired Markups and Prices in Economies under Adjustment

We can now move from these comments on the general implications of adjustment to a particular form of the general formula on desired markups and prices which is appropriate for studying the dynamics of inflation in countries undergoing adjustment and affected by the other conditions listed above. As already outlined, an economy under adjustment tends to set economic policy so as to increase foreign trade surpluses, control the net inflow/outflow of external/internal funds, and reduce the public-sector deficit. These policies tend to impart critical importance to the prices of products which contain a large amount of imported inputs and/or are intensely used in the production of exportable goods.[15] This impact is due to the specific undersupply of such goods because of import controls, whose intensification is expected at every level, or to expectations of significant real currency devaluations designed to encourage exports and inhibit imports. The need to reduce the fiscal deficit associated with the financial fragility of the public sector means that the user cost of public-fiscal goods becomes an important factor in determining desired markups, especially in sectors that make intensive use of such goods.

For this reason, when the object of study is the dynamics of inflation in economies of the type to which I have been referring, it is important to work with expressions for desired markups and prices that include three types of input: public-fiscal goods, exchange goods, and other goods. Thus the particular form of the general formula given in chapter 4 for the cases to be examined here can be arrived at by substituting for the term which refers to the contribution of raw materials to desired markups an expression representing these three types of input.[16] Thus, assuming that:

$$(1-f)\rho_m = e \cdot \rho_e + l \cdot \rho_l + o \cdot \rho_o \qquad (1)$$

where:

e is the cost of the exchange goods utilized as inputs as a proportion of c;

l is the cost of the public-fiscal goods utilized as inputs as a proportion of c;

o is the cost of the other goods utilized as inputs as a proportion of c;

ρ_e is the maximum rate at which the prices of exchange goods are expected to rise in real terms;

ρ_l is the maximum rate at which the prices of public-fiscal goods are expected to rise in real terms;

ρ_o is the maximum rate at which the prices of other inputs are expected to rise in real terms;

and substituting expression (1) for the term $(1-f)\cdot\rho_m$ in the general formula for desired markups, we have:

$$z = (f + e\cdot\rho_e + l\cdot\rho_l + o\cdot\rho_o + y\cdot\rho_k + m^*)/(1 - h\cdot k/v) - 1 \quad (2)$$

Expression (2) is the general formula adapted to the study of desired markups in economies undergoing adjustment.

If we multiply this term for desired markups by direct costs, we obtain the general formula for analysis of the behavior of prices in such economies:

$$p = (f + e\cdot\rho_e + l\cdot\rho_l + o\cdot\rho_o + y\cdot\rho_k + m^*)\cdot (wb + p_e\cdot e^* + p_l\cdot l^* + p_o\cdot o^*)/(1 - h\cdot k/v) \quad (3)$$

where:

p_e is the current price of the exchange goods utilized as inputs;

p_l is the current price of the public-fiscal goods utilized as inputs;

p_o is the current price of the other goods utilized as inputs;

e^* is the coefficient of utilization of exchange goods per unit of output;

l^* is the coefficient of utilization of public-fiscal goods per unit of output;

o^* is the coefficient of utilization of other goods per unit of output.

These expressions formalize a theoretical framework with which it is possible analytically to counterpose the various aspects that affect the short-run dynamics of desired markups and prices. These aspects include variations in all kinds of current direct costs, in expectations about levels of capacity utilization, in the need to increase desired markups so as to alter the composition of investment funding, and in the user cost of the various items of producer goods.

However, exercises such as these in specific analysis do not fall within the scope of the present study. My objective here is developing a theoretical framework for analyzing short-run variations in desired markups and prices under conditions of adjustment, and demonstrating that the imposition of adjustment in economies with the characteristics defined above leads to two consequences: desired markups higher than they would be in a situation of low instability, given that values of ρ_e and/or ρ_l are greater than 1; and principally, pressure for changes in relative prices among sectors with differing structures of productive consumption of exchange goods and public-fiscal goods. This pressure tends to persist for as long as the financial fragility of the public sector persists. More precisely, recognition of the fact that the economies under scrutiny here have a structure"[17]—i.e., that they are economies which make products with significantly differentiated compositions of inputs–represents from the analytical standpoint the interaction between several price equations with different values of e, l, and y.

As a result, in a situation of adjustment, desired markups tend to change in a differentiated manner, depending on the differing importance of exchange goods and public-fiscal goods in each sector. Consequently, in economies under adjustment, there are pressures for changes in relative prices among sectors with differing compositions of inputs in terms of exchange goods and public-fiscal goods. This pressure for changes in relative prices, in an economy where the prevailing mechanism of propagation is based on the complete transfer of past inflation into the present, causes an acceleration of inflation which is sustained until the adjustment is considered complete.[18]

In what follows I develop a model to show that in cases where the changes in public-sector liabilities caused by adjustment processes reach the point of producing a situation of fragility in the public finances, the acceleration of inflation begins to incorporate an endogenous element.

6

THE ENDOGENOUS COMPONENT IN THE ACCELERATION OF INFLATION

6.1 Introduction

As shown in chapter 5, an economy undergoing adjustment is subject to inflation shocks resulting from the direct impacts of adjustment processes.[1] In addition to these shocks, which are usually the ones highlighted in analyses of specific manifestations of the acceleration of inflation in countries with the characteristics described in the preceding chapter, there are also indirect impacts whose dynamics require greater theoretical development.

It is possible to develop a theoretical demonstration of the tendency to endogenization of the acceleration of inflation that occurs under certain circumstances. I contend that the economies in question present, in addition to the inertial component which is inherent in chronically inflationary economies,[2] an autonomous component of acceleration which manifests itself when the financial situation of the public sector is fragile.

As pointed out at the end of the last chapter, the perception that adjustment has not been concluded together with the fact that economies have a "structure" tends to make inflation accelerate in chronically inflationary economies. In what follows I use a model to show that when adjustment processes lead to such expressive changes in the liabilities of the public sector as to induce fragility in the public finances, the acceleration caused by differences in desired markups between sectors tends to be sustained because of the interaction of several processes, among which the most important are acceleration of inflation, the financial fragility of the public sector, and the increase in the user cost of public-fiscal goods.

To demonstrate this, the first step will be to present a simplified model of inflation designed to highlight the role played by the user-cost index of public-fiscal goods in the dynamics of inflation. Next, the basic determinants of the user-cost index of these goods will be discussed, after which each of these determinants will be analyzed to pave the way for presenting a model representing the basic interactions between the acceleration of inflation, the financial fragility of the public sector, and the user-cost index of public-fiscal goods. The chapter concludes with a demonstration of the effects and limits of some types of economic policy that have been used to contain the acceleration or to reduce the inflation rate itself.

6.2 A Simple Model of Inflation

In a chronically inflationary economy, the dynamics of inflation follows the general model below:

$$I_t = r \cdot I_{t-1} + A \qquad (1)$$

where:

- I_t is the inflation rate in the period t;
- r is a coefficient which depends on the implementation of a policy of freezing or controlling prices and incomes $(o < r < 1)$;
- A is a term for the acceleration of the inflation.

Thus when $r = 1$, i.e., when no attempt is made to control or freeze prices and incomes, chronically inflationary economies tend to have a basic inflation rate corresponding to the inertial component of inflation, whose logic was explained by the neostructuralists.[3] In addition to the inertial component, which is qualified by the relative degree of the price freeze or control policy, inflation is determined by an acceleration component whose principal characteristics will be analyzed in this chapter by building on the theoretical discussion in chapters 4 and 5 regarding the behavior of desired markups.[4]

Since it is not my intention to examine all the determinants of this acceleration but merely to give a theoretical demonstration that under certain circumstances the financial fragility of the public sector, associated with other elements, tends to endogenize the acceleration of inflation, I make use of a model comprising four elements: typically exogenous inflationary shocks, the user-cost index of public-fiscal goods, the productive structure, and, finally, what I term secondary elements.[5]

The inflation model presented above can be rewritten as:

$$I_t = r \cdot I_{t-1} + A(ES, \rho_l, SE)/\& \qquad (2)$$

where:

ES is the inflationary shocks caused by direct impacts;
ρ_l is the user-cost index of public-fiscal goods;
SE represents the action of secondary elements;
$\&$ represents the productive structure.[6]

When ρ_l is greater than 1 inflation will be accelerating for the reasons outlined in the preceding chapter, provided there are no opposing forces (ES) which (as we will see) can often decelerate inflation in the short run at the cost of reaccelerating it later on.

The next item presents the basic determinants of ρ_l,[7] followed by an examination of the main dynamic aspects of these determinants. Once the dynamic aspects of the basic determinants of ρ_l have been established, it will at last be possible to put forward a model representing the interactions between the financial fragility of the public sector, the user-cost index of public-fiscal goods, and the acceleration of inflation.

6.3 Relations between the Acceleration of Inflation and the User-Cost Index of Public-Fiscal Goods

It is possible to represent the relationship between the user-cost index of public-fiscal goods and inflation through a function that simplifies the acceleration component represented by expression (2):

$$A = A(a, \rho_l) \qquad (3)$$

where:

ρ_l is greater than or equal to 1;
A is the acceleration of inflation;

a is the other determinants of acceleration (ES, &, SE).

Generally speaking, the greater the user-cost index of public-fiscal goods (ρ_l), the greater will be the rate at which inflation accelerates. The greater the disequilibrium between the financial obligations to be paid by government and its net revenues (net tax collections plus profits of state-owned corporations), i.e., the greater the intensity of the real expected increase in prices, charges, and taxes, and the expected cut in subsidies required to overcome the financial fragility of the public sector, the greater will be the user-cost index of public-fiscal goods (ρ_l) and hence the greater the pressures for the acceleration of inflation.[8] In like manner, for the same perception of the financial situation of the public sector, the acceleration of inflation will be the greater the more the other determinants of inflation rise—and this means all the determinants related to typically exogenous inflationary shocks and to secondary elements. This is represented graphically in figure 11, showing different curves AG (relations between the user-cost index of public-fiscal goods and the acceleration of inflation) depending on the other determinants of the acceleration.

Before discussing the determinants of the user-cost index of public-fiscal goods (ρ_l), I want to highlight some points regarding the possible courses for economic policy to take and for inflation to accelerate which tend to occur when the inflation rate is high and the financial maladjustment of the public sector is considerable—these trajectories are shown in figures 12 and 13.[9]

When inflation is high, governments usually make recurrent financial concessions to keep inflation under control. This fact tends to be accompanied by an increase in the user-cost index of public-fiscal goods (as will be shown below) and this increase in turn tends to accelerate inflation at a later point in time. The situation can be represented in figures 12 and 13 as upward movements along one of the AG curves. In addition, the constant deterioration in the financial position of the public sector tends to reach a limit in the capacity of the economic system to absorb the growing volumes of credit

Figure 11

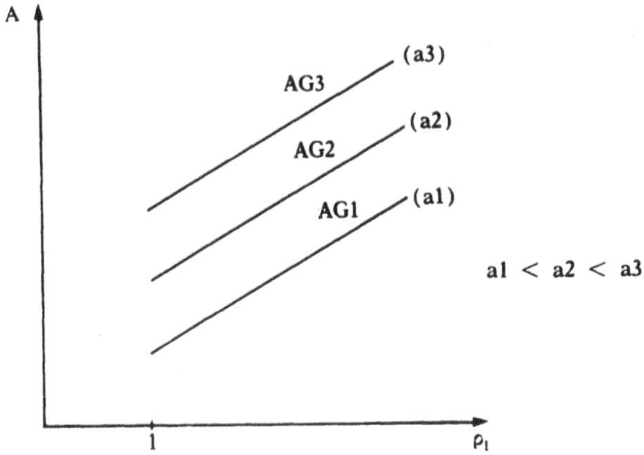

Figure 12

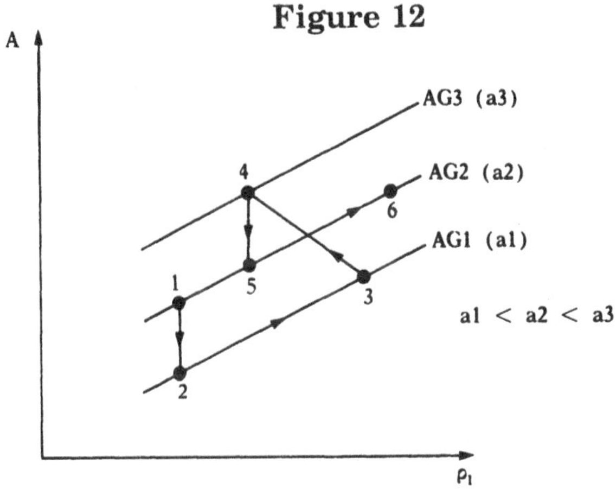

Figure 13

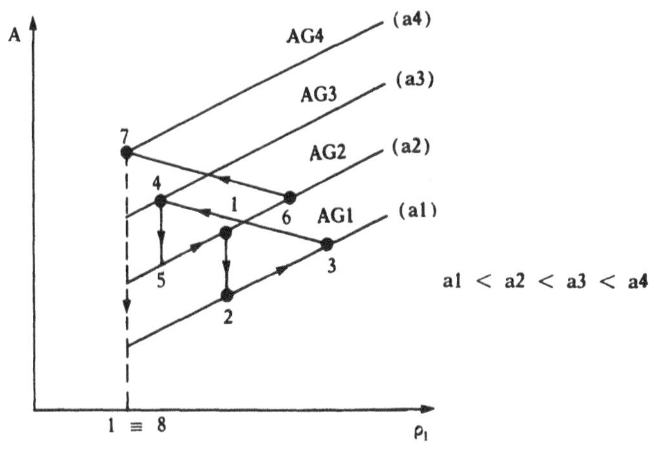

operations with the private sector which such policies eventually entail. Sooner or later the government is obliged to seek a fiscal adjustment that directly affects prices (increased or rates in public goods and/or cuts in subsidies and transfers). Following a persistent rise, ρ_l tends to fall back again at the cost of increasing the acceleration of inflation caused by a fiscal shock or by a change in the value of a.

In terms of figures 12 and 13, it can be seen that the curve AG is shifted upwards, and that the greater the fiscal shock introduced by government the greater the shift will be. This process of fiscal adjustment and acceleration of inflation can be divergent (fig. 12) or convergent (fig. 13), depending on the level of public-sector financial maladjustment, the other determinants of inflation, and the political conditions for implementing the required fiscal adjustments. An analysis of this question is included in the discussion which concludes this chapter.

6.4 The Determinants of the User-Cost Index of Public-Fiscal Goods

As I have already pointed out, a situation of maladjustment can be translated by values greater than 1 for the user-cost index of public-fiscal goods and exchange goods, i.e., $\rho_l > 1$ and $\rho_e > 1$. In cases where the financial situation of the public sector is sufficiently sound to absorb the acceleration caused by such user-cost index values through financial concessions, the adjustments can be made and the values of ρ_l and ρ_e return to 1 once again. However, adjustment processes tend to transform significantly the financial situation of the public-sector, leading to the formation of extremely large public debts. These debts create financial obligations of such magnitude that expectations of fiscal adjustments become recurrent in view of the virtual impossibility of expanding the financial of this debt in an inexpensive manner under the conditions of instability typical of adjustment periods. When adjustment processes lead to a situation of public-sector financial fragility, the user-cost index of public-fiscal goods becomes systematically greater than 1 as a reflection of this fragility. Under such conditions, a government has no alternative sources of financing to enable it to meet its future financial commitments without considerably incrementing its financial costs. Identification of this situation with a user-cost index of public-fiscal goods greater than 1 represents recognition of the need for a fiscal adjustment. The more fragile the financial situation of the public sector is considered, the more drastic the adjustment need be.

An analytical expression for the determinants of variations in public-sector financial fragility, hence of ρ_l, will make it possible to study the dynamics of this term. I assume that the user-cost index of public-fiscal goods increases as the financial fragility of the public sector $(b \cdot F_g)$ increases,[10] and that autonomous variations may also occur because of the perception that the government might implement adjustments more drastic than those required to stabilize this fragility. Under conditions of adjustment an increasing degree of public-sector financial fragility leads to a need for a bigger fiscal adjustment, and hence potentially faster acceleration. If it were not for the objective necessity of adjustment, however, it would be possible to envisage a rising correlation between the government's financial obligations and its generation of funds without the inevitable consequence of increasing inflationary pressure.[11] Thus in an economy with a financially fragile public sector the user-cost index of public-fiscal goods and the government's financial fragility could be defined in accordance with the following expressions:

$$\rho_l = b \cdot F_g + d \tag{4}$$

where:

ρ_l is greater than or equal to 1;
d is greater than or equal to zero;
b is greater than zero;

$$F_g = (j \cdot D)/(c \cdot X) \tag{5}$$

where:

F_g is the relation between the government's financial expenditure and its net revenue;
j is the average cost of the total public debt;

D is the total public debt;

b is a parameter which depends on the conditions for financing the public sector and which varies in accordance with the particular conditions in each economy and each situation;[12]

d is a term for expectations, which assumes values greater than zero when, despite a stable situation of public-sector financial fragility, a fiscal reinforcement is expected;

X is the product of the economy;

c is the average net revenue of the public sector per unit of output, defined here as the sum of the net tax per product (tax minus subsidies and transfers) and the profit per product of the state-owned enterprises.

My hypothesis is that the user-cost index of public-fiscal goods increases as public-sector financial fragility increases. This fragility can be measured by a coefficient which correlates the financial cost of the total public debt ($j \cdot D$) with the total net revenue of the public sector ($c \cdot X$), in the context of a given scheme for financing the public sector (b). This means, for example, that if the net tax burden per unit of output and/or the prices of public goods decrease in real terms, there will be a reduction in the value of c, which, all other things being equal, will in turn raise the values of F_g and ρ_l. To facilitate the study of the dynamic determinants of ρ_l, let us divide the formula for F_g into parts:

$$\rho_l = (b \cdot j/c) \cdot (D/X) + d \qquad (6)$$

Expression (6) tells us that ρ_l depends on:

(a) the ratio of the average cost of total public debt to the average net public-sector revenue per unit of output (j/c);

(b) the total public debt per unit of output (D/X);

(c) parameter b, which reflects the conditions for public-sector financing;

(d) an autonomous term d, whose movements are sporadic and, from the standpoint of this analysis, relevant only in situations where public-sector financial fragility is stable.

Figure 14

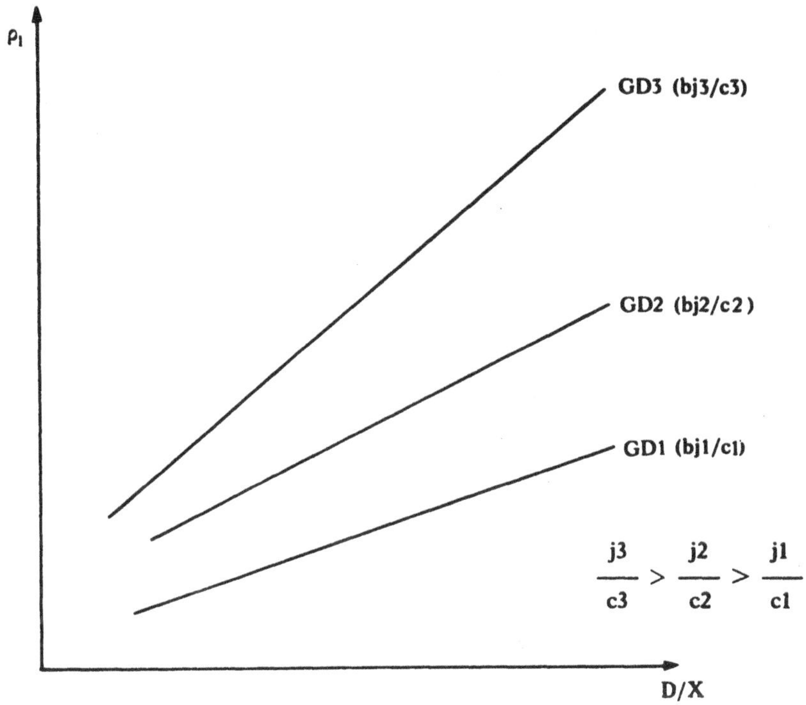

Figure 15

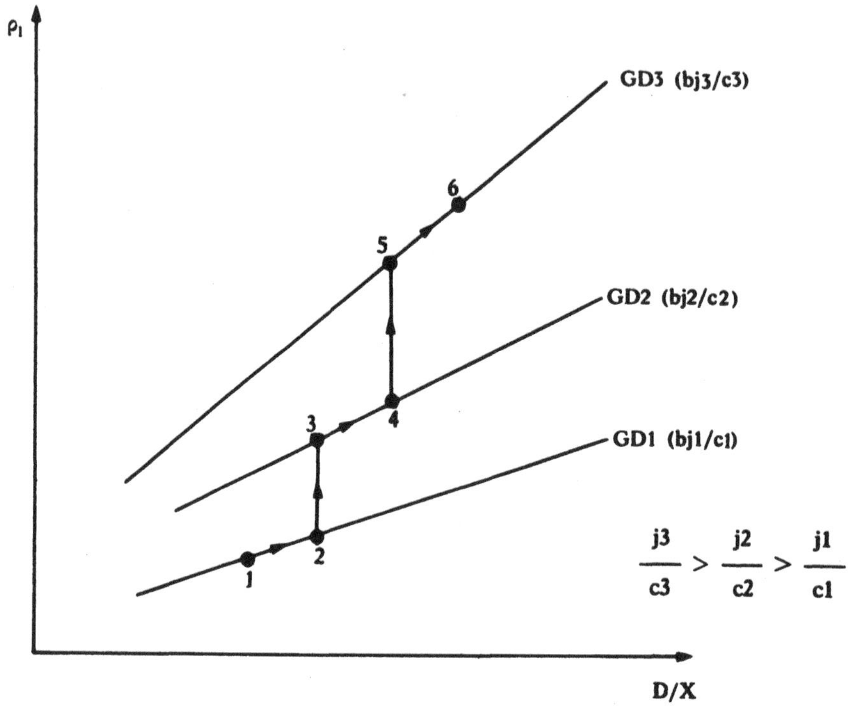

ρ_1
GD3 (bj3/c3)
GD2 (bj2/c2)
GD1 (bj1/c1)
1
2
3
4
5
6
$\frac{j3}{c3} > \frac{j2}{c2} > \frac{j1}{c1}$
D/X

For the purposes of this discussion, it is useful to represent these relations in graphic form. Figure 14 shows that the user-cost index of public-fiscal goods (ρ_l) has a linear relation to D/X, and that its angular coefficient is parameter b multiplied by the ratio j/c. For a given ratio $b \cdot j/c$, the bigger the total public debt per unit of output the bigger ρ_l will be.[13] On the other hand, the higher the ratio $b \cdot j/c$ (i.e., the higher the average cost of total debt in relation to average net public-sector revenue per unit of output given a financing scheme b) the greater ρ_l will be for the same level of D/X.

Before discussing the determinants of D/X and $b \cdot j/c$, it is worth making a brief digression, as an introduction to the dynamic analysis developed below. Regarding one of the common ways in which the relation between ρ_l and D/X unfolds under conditions of adjustment.

Figure 15 shows a situation which has been typical of economies subjected to adjustment. As already remarked, the aggravation in the conditions for recycling the foreign debt leads to heavy public-sector indebtedness. Thus economies under adjustment have usually begun their *via crucis* with a high ratio of total public debt to public-sector operating surplus.[14] As I will show in the following section, when the public-sector operating surplus per unit of output is below a given critical level, the total public debt per unit of output (D/X) tends to increase. In figure 15, this means an upward shift in ρ_l along the curve GD.

With the increase in the ratio D/X, there tends to be pressure for an increase in the interest rate paid by the public sector, and/or a reduction in the maturity of the public debt. If no corresponding fiscal adjustment is forthcoming, there will be an increase in the ratio $b \cdot j/c$, meaning that every time D/X increases there will be a more intense increase in ρ_l compared with the previous situation, and this in turn will tend to push the inflation rate up even faster. If government reacts to this acceleration by holding down the prices of public goods, there will be an even bigger increase in the ratio $b \cdot j/c$, which will once again refuel the acceleration of inflation.

We now begin our study of the determinants of the evolution of ρ_l, taking each of its component parts separately.

6.5 The Determinants of Total Public-Sector Debt per Unit of Output (*D/X*)

To begin this study of the determinants of total public-sector debt per unit of output, it is useful to take an identity representing the government's budget constraints as a single consolidated entity, including the monetary authorities:

$$j - s = d - d^{-1} \cdot (1 + p) + m - m^{-1} \tag{7}$$

where:

j is the net interest paid by the public sector on its debt;
s is the operating or non-financial surplus of the public sector;
d is total (internal and external) public-sector debt;
m is the money supply;
p is the inflation rate.

If the net interest paid by government depends only on the total public-sector debt from the previous period and the government executes a passive monetary policy,[15] then:

$$j = r \cdot (1 + p) \cdot d^{-1} \tag{8}$$
$$m = m^{-1} \cdot (1 + p) \cdot (1 + q) \tag{9}$$

where:

r is the average real cost of the total public-sector debt;
q is the rate of growth of output.

Insertion of (8) and (9) in (7) leads to:

$$r(1+p)d^{-1} - s = d - d^{-1} \cdot (1+p) + m^{-1}[(1+p) \cdot (1+q) - 1] \tag{10}$$

which when algebraically rearranged becomes:

$$d = d^{-1}[(1+p) \cdot (1+r)] - m^{-1}[(1+p) \cdot (1+q) - 1] - s \tag{11}$$

Assuming that the general price level in a period is the general price level of the previous multiplied by $(1 + p)$, and dividing all the terms by the general price level, the result is:

$$D = D^{-1}(1+r) - M^{-1}[(1+q) - 1/(1+p)] - S \tag{12}$$

where:

> D, M, and S correspond to the values of d, m, and s expressed in real terms.

Since the aim here is to study the determinants of D/X, let us divide all the terms of expression (12) by X (total output) and let $X = X^{-1} \cdot (1+q)$. Thus:

$$D/X = (D^{-1}/X^{-1})[(1+r)/(1+q)] - M^{-1}/X^{-1} \{1 - 1/[(1+p)(1+q)]\} - S/X \quad (13)$$

To facilitate understanding of the factors that affect the evolution of D/X, we divide all the members of expression (13) by D^{-1}/X^{-1}, thus leading to:

$$(D/X)/(D^{-1}/X^{-1}) = (1+r)/(1+q) - M^{-1}/D^{-1}\{1 - 1/[(1+p)(1+q)]\} - (S/X)/(D^{-1}/X^{-1}) \quad (14)$$

This expression suggests that the evolution of D/X depends on three factors:

(a) the ratio of the rate of output growth to the rate of growth in the average real cost of total public debt;[16]
(b) inflation tax;
(c) the ratio of operating public-sector surplus to total public debt per unit of output in the preceding period.

If in a context of adjustment the relation between interest rates and economic growth tends to stay relatively steady because economic policy has very little room for maneuver, the evolution of D/X will depend fundamentally on the evolution of the inflation rate and of the ratio between the public-sector operating surplus and the past stock of public debt.

Inflation is one way of financing the public sector through what is termed "inflation tax"; the more demand there is for money in the economy and the higher the inflation rate, the higher inflation tax will be. But the demand for money varies inversely with the inflation rate, so that inflation tax depends on two contradictory forces. When the inflation rate rises, inflation tax also rises, provided that its reduction, corresponding to a fall in the desire to hold money, does not cancel out the effect of the rise in the inflation rate. From this point on, inflation tax begins to fall as inflation rises:

> A rise in the inflation rate does not necessarily benefit the government in terms of inflation tax, for it may be more than offset by a drop in demand for money. (Marfán 1986, 112).[17]

In these cases of chronically inflationary economies undergoing adjustment, and hence with high public-sector indebtedness, the role of inflation in containing the evolution of D/X tends to be not only a minor one but also one which declines with the acceleration of inflation.

Let us now turn to the effect of the ratio of the public-sector operating surplus per unit of output (S/X) to total public debt per unit of output in the preceding period (D^{-1}/X^{-1}) on the evolution of D/X. For this purpose, we can return to expression (13), which can be understood as an inverse correlation between D/X and S/X. This in turn can be represented graphically as a straight line, as shown in figure 16, with an angular coefficient equal to -1 and a point of intercept equal to:

$$(D^{-1}/X^{-1})[(1+r)/(1+q)]- M^{-1}/X^{-1}\{1-1/[(1+p)\cdot(1+q)]\} \qquad (15)$$

This tells us that the greater the total public debt per unit of output in the preceding period, the higher the intercept point will be. It also shows that depending on the value of S/X, that of D/X will be greater than, smaller than, or equal to D^{-1}/X^{-1}. To know what value of S/X will lead to a rising value of D/X, it suffices to find out under what conditions:

$$D/X - D^{-1}/X^{-1} > 0 \qquad (16)$$

To know what factors condition a rise in the net public debt per unit of output, it suffices to subtract D^{-1}/X^{-1} from the second member of expression (13) and impose the condition expressed in (16). Thus, D/X will exceed D^{-1}/X^{-1} provided that:

$$(D^{-1}/X^{-1})[(1+r)/(1+q)] - M^{-1}/X^{-1}\{1-1/[(1+p)(1+q)]\} - S/X - D^{-1}/X^{-1} > 0 \qquad (17)$$

Figure 16

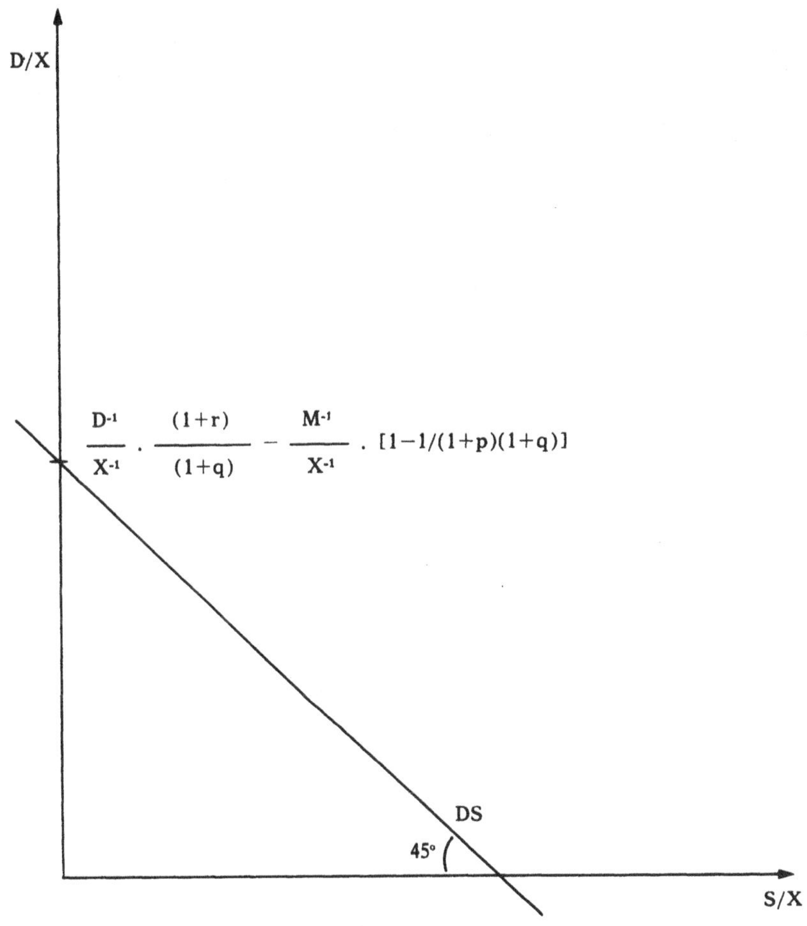

which with some algebraic transformations can be expressed as:

$$(D^{-1}/X^{-1})[(r-q)/(l+q)] - M^{-1}/X^{-1}\{1-1/[(1+p)(1+q)]\} > S/X \tag{18}$$

Thus, if the operating surplus per unit of output is smaller than the value of the critical primary surplus corresponding to the first member of expression (18), the result will be a situation in which D/X increases. In terms of the preceding figure, the evolution of total public debt can be synthetically represented as in figures 17 and 18. If an economy is in region 1 of figure 17, i.e., if S/X is below its critical value (corresponding to the lefthand side of expression 17), there will be a gradual shift of the curve as the value of D/X increases, as shown in figure 18. This observation will be useful when we discuss the dynamics of inflation under conditions of public-sector financial fragility, which corresponds to a primary public-sector surplus below its critical value in a context where the conditions for financing are not adequate—a typical situation in economies under adjustment.

6.6 The Determinants of the Relation between Average Cost of the Total Public Debt and Net Public-Sector Revenue

As already stressed, my concern is to study the dynamics of inflation in chronically inflationary economies undergoing adjustment and with a financially fragile public sector. I contend that under such conditions interest rates tend to be reasonably resistant to downward pressure.[18] I explain why in what follows.

As shown in chapter 5, in a context of adjustment uncertainty about the future, values of exchange goods and public-fiscal goods tend to accelerate inflation owing to variations in desired markups. The acceleration of inflation in turn tends to create many problems for the financial system, most of them multi-correlated.[19] Among these problems, the following are especially important:

(a) increased uncertainty about inflation;

(b) curtailment of the implicit maturities in credit and investment contracts;[20]
(c) increases in the risk premiums or spreads demanded by investors;
(d) increased fragility of the financial system;[21]
(e) tendency for financial disintermediation to increase;
(f) tendency for capital flight to increase.

A combination of items (b) and (c) tends to cause a mismatch between the assets and liabilities of financial institutions, and this in turn tends to make the whole process still worse. As the instability deepens, the bankruptcy of one or another institution is both a strong probability and a further boost to all the trends involved in the process.

As an alternative to the scenario outlined above, the government might attempt to control the process by issuing regulations on maturities and rates for financial transactions to protect institutions from such a mismatch. While government can do this to a certain extent, its scope for maneuver is relatively narrow because of the risks of financial disintermediation and/or capital flight. In its efforts to avoid such an outcome—or rather, to minimize these consequences, which are virtually inevitable—government is forced to limit its interventions through regulation of maturities and rates for financial transactions, and hence to look on while financial institutions are undermined by accelerating inflation.

To prevent this undermining from becoming a financial crisis—or more precisely, to postpone such a crisis as long as possible—governments end up being forced not only to permit interest rates to remain high as a way of keeping investors in the system, but to bail financial institutions out by means of a whole series of expedients which, from the standpoint of the analytical schema used here, reduce the value of c.[22] Government is obliged to proceed in this manner, for otherwise it would have to run two risks: (a) under normal circumstances the deterioration in financial institutions would tend to produce financial disintermediation with serious consequences both from the standpoint of immediate economic stability, caused by a run on the banks, and in terms of an even greater acceleration of inflation; (b) under conditions of

Figure 17

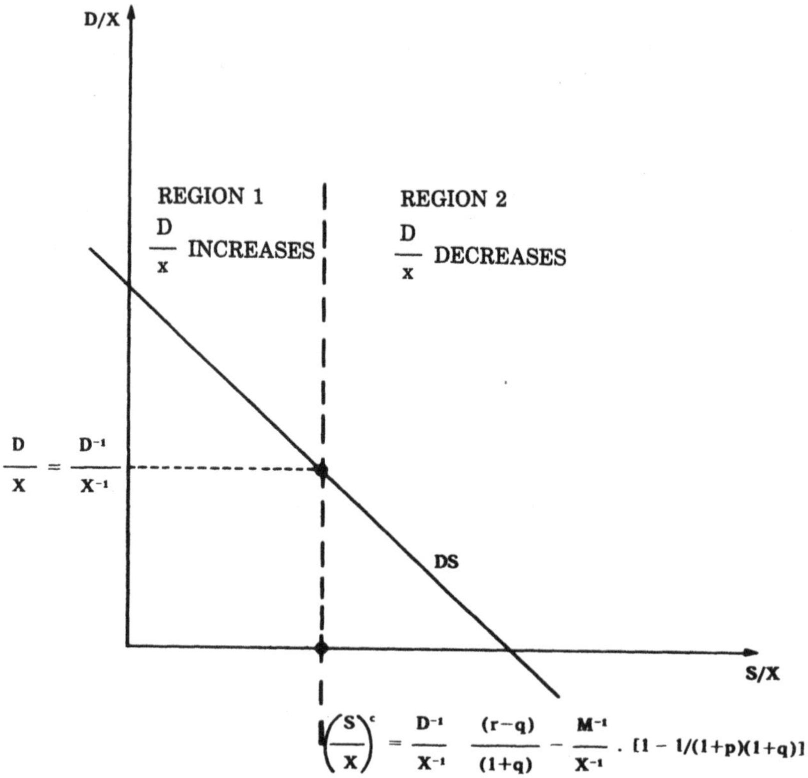

where $(\frac{S}{X})^C$ is the critical value of $\frac{S}{X}$

Figure 18

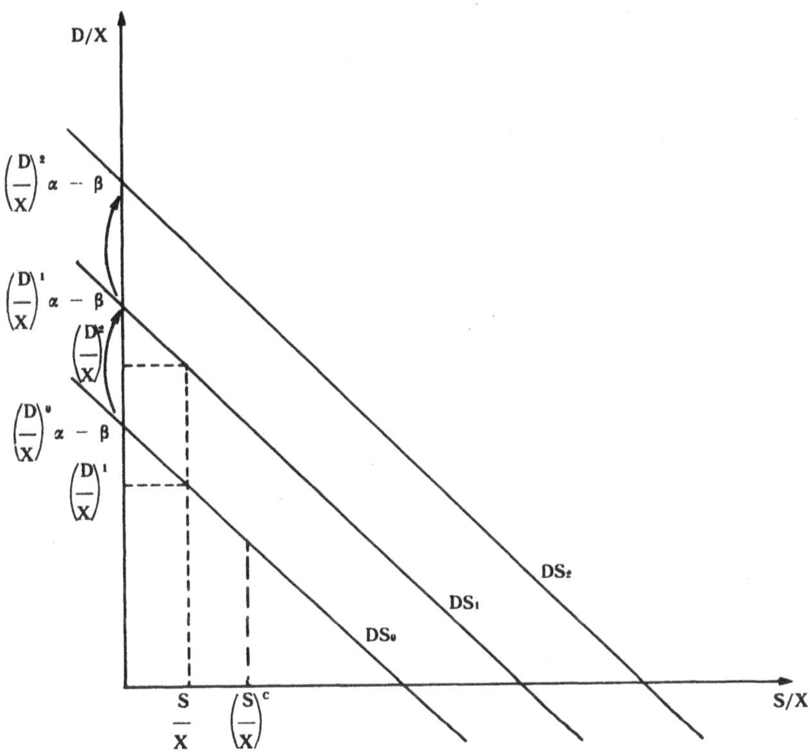

where:

$$\alpha = \frac{1+r}{1+q}$$

$$\beta = \frac{M^{-1}}{X^{-1}} + [1 - 1/(1+p)(1+q)]$$

adjustment, when international interest rates are high, there is the further risk of capital flight, with the additional negative effects of instability on the parallel foreign exchange market and, by the same token, fluctuating foreign currency earnings due to the adverse effects of significant differences between official and informal exchange rates on foreign trade.

To prevent both financial disintermediation and capital flight, governments tend to:

(a) avoid a financial crisis by making many concessions to financial intermediaries and/or final debtors in precarious financial conditions, thereby strengthening them and greatly jeopardizing the average net revenues of the public sector c;

(b) permit stabilization of interest rates at high levels or allow them to rise still further, which affects the average cost of the total public debt j.

If government is unwilling or unable, for financial or political reasons, to increase financial concessions in favor of the financial system or the strongly indebted firms which could affect the financial system, it will be forced to bear the costs of a rise in j. If, on the contrary, interest rates cannot be kept high, for political reasons or because this would seriously damage important firms in a delicate financial situation, government will be obliged to strongly jeopardize its own net revenue per unit of output c.

All this leads to the conclusion that an acceleration of inflation in a fragile financial system increases the probability that a financial crisis will occur and hence eventually makes governments take a series of defensive measures to avoid a crisis. No matter how these measures are designed, they ultimately produce an increase in the ratio between the average cost of the total public debt and the net revenue of the public sector (j/c).

6.7 A Model Representing the Basic Interactions in the Acceleration of Inflation

To analyze the basic interactions in acceleration, i.e., the interactions between the user cost of public-fiscal goods, the acceleration, and the determinants of public-sector financial fragility, I shall proceed to an analytical integration of the three ratios discussed above with a fourth, which will be discussed below, using a model represented in static terms in figure 19.[23]

This analytical model contains all three ratios, represented by curves AG, DS, and GD, as well as a fourth, curve SA. This new curve tells us that if no acceleration occurs, the public-sector primary surplus will remain steady at its initial value, which is equal to the intercept of curve SA with axis S/X. If on the contrary inflation does accelerate, the public-sector primary surplus is reduced, leading curve SA to move to the right. The more inflation accelerates, the more the surplus is reduced and the further the curve shifts to the right.[24]

In addition to showing these four curves, figure 19 highlights the fact that if the primary surplus per unit of output (S/X) is equal to its critical ratio (as defined in the section on the determinants of the evolution of the total public debt per unit of output), D/X will remain stable, as will the value of ρ_l. If the initial value of ρ_l is equal to 1, S/X will remain equal to its critical ratio, which in turn will tend to maintain the stability of D/X and ρ_l.

However, this is not the situation of a complex economy undergoing adjustment that has a financially fragile public sector. As I have stressed, the external adjustment process tends to lead to a situation of excessive public-sector indebtedness, and hence to a ratio of S/X which is at least very close to, if not actually below, its critical level. In association with this, the actual need for external adjustment and uncertainty about the external accounts tend to accelerate the inflation rate because of uncertainty about the user cost of exchange goods. This acceleration of inflation tends to diminish the value of S/X,[25] and together with the high level of initial indebtedness this intensifies the difference between the ratio S/X and its critical level. Moreover, the acceleration of inflation tends to raise the ratio $b \cdot j/c$, thereby increasing the negative effects of a rising ratio of debt to output on the acceleration. This series of processes tends to keep inflation accelerating and makes it more and more difficult to handle

Figure 19

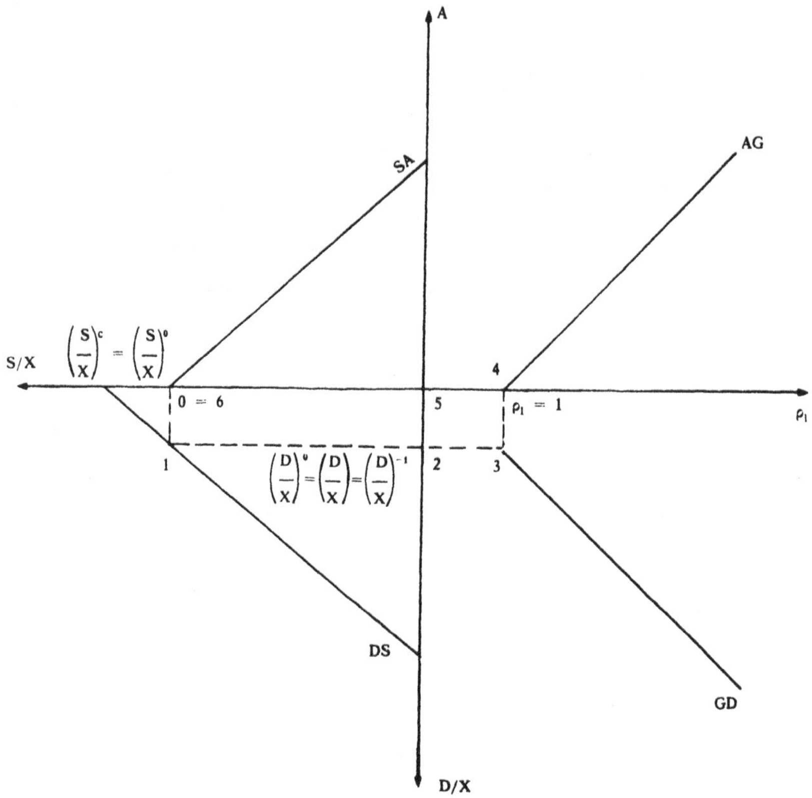
A
SA
AG
S/X
$\left(\frac{S}{X}\right)^c = \left(\frac{S}{X}\right)^0$
4
0 = 6
5
$\rho_1 = 1$
ρ_1
1
$\left(\frac{D}{X}\right)^0 = \left(\frac{D}{X}\right) = \left(\frac{D}{X}\right)^{-1}$
2
3
DS
GD
D/X

economic policy making. In what follows these points are examined in more detail.

The dynamics of acceleration in an economy with the characteristics in question, and assuming a passive governmental attitude for the time being, could be represented as in figures 23 and 24. These figures synthesize the consequences of the dynamic relations implicit in the curves SA, DS, and GD for a situation in which S/X is below its critical level. In order to clarify the various aspects of these dynamics, I shall first show through figures 20, 21, and 22 the role each of these relationships would play in a hypothetical situation where the dynamic mechanisms of the other two relationships were sterilized.

Figure 20 shows the dynamic effects of curve DS in a situation where S/X is lower than its critical value. I have assumed for ease of exposition that curve SA is vertical and the angular coefficient corresponding to curve GD is stable. In other words, it is assumed that the ratios S/X and $b \cdot j/c$ are insensitive to the acceleration of inflation. Under such conditions an initial ratio of S/X below the critical value (0)[26] would, through curve DS, determine a higher value of debt per unit of output than for the preceding period (1, 2). This fact would have two consequences. First there would be a rise in ρ_l (2, 4, 5) which, through curve AG, would finally lead to an acceleration of inflation (6, 7). Second, and this is one of the dynamic aspects I wish to highlight, the rise in D/X would entail a shift in curve DS (3), since—as we saw in the analysis of the determinants of the evolution of total public debt per unit of output—the point of intercept of this curve depends on the value of D/X in the preceding period. Thus, even in a hypothetical situation where S/X and $b \cdot j/c$ were constant, if S/X is below its critical level a gradual rise in the total public debt per unit of output would result. Hence, if all other factors remained constant, a rise in the user-cost index of public fiscal goods would occur.

Consequently, in an economy with the above-mentioned conditions, an initial situation with S/X below its critical level would be enough to result in a gradual rise in D/X, which would manifest itself as a gradual shift in curve DS. This movement of D/X would lead to a similarly gradual

Figure 20

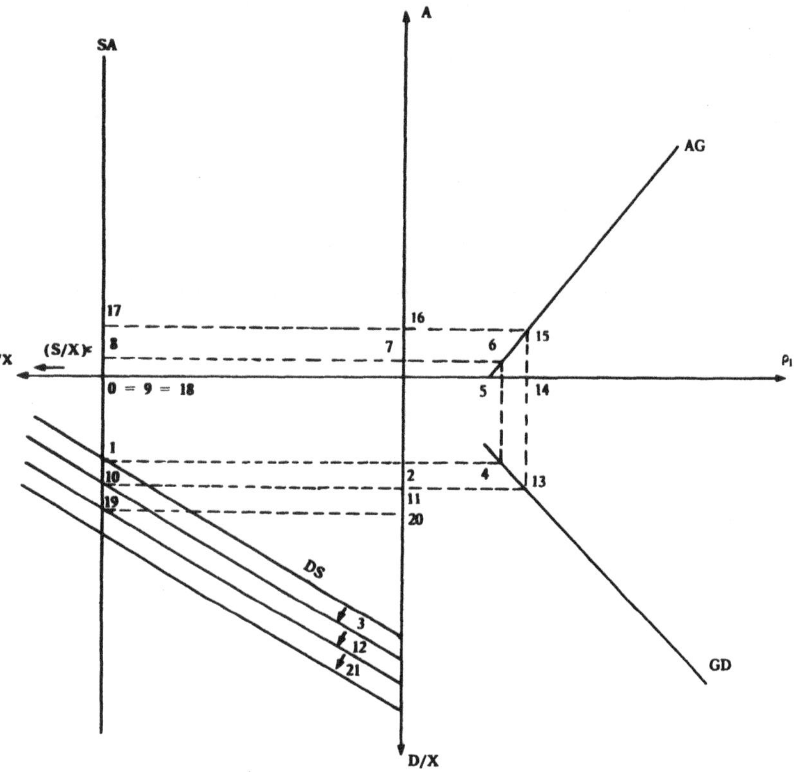
A
SA
AG
17
16
15
(S/X)*
8
7
6
S/X
P1
0 = 9 = 18
5
14
1
10
2
4
13
19
11
20
Ds
3
12
21
GD
D/X

increase in the user-cost index of public-fiscal goods, which in turn would represent intensifying pressure on inflation to accelerate. This is one of the basic processes in what I have been referring to as the endogenous component in acceleration.[27]

But to have a more complex, concrete view of the dynamics of inflation, its other aspects must be brought into the limelight. First, we need to examine the main consequences of acceleration from the standpoint of the analysis which is being conducted here. Only then can we logically discuss economic policy measures governments tend to introduce in order to improve the public-sector financial situation and to take the sting out of the spurts in acceleration and their implications. I turn to this task in the next section.

There are two types of impacts of acceleration; those which are external and those internal to the model presented. By external impacts I mean that acceleration tends to cause a great many reactions which multiply the initial acceleration, such as attempts to shorten intervals between adjustment of prices and incomes,[28] or all the other kinds of reaction indicated above which I have called secondary elements in the acceleration of inflation. I shall leave aside these latter effects, as in an immediate sense they merely act to multiply or give a fresh boost to the basic processes which are being described here; and I shall now comment on the consequences of acceleration in terms of the model presented above.

From the standpoint of the model, an acceleration of inflation tends to have three important consequences: reduction of the public-sector operating surplus per unit of product, S/X; an increase in the ratio of the average cost of total public debt to average public-sector revenue per unit of output, j/c; and deterioration in the conditions for financing the public sector, i.e., a rise in b. Figures 21 and 22 show the dynamic implications of all three.

Figure 21 presents the dynamic effects of a low ratio S/X in a situation where curve SA is no longer vertical. It allows us to examine the dynamic effects of the interaction between rates of acceleration and S/X. Since my objective here is to highlight this latter interaction, I shall assume that the relations implicit in curves DS and GD are stable. Under such conditions, a ratio S/X below its critical level (0) leads to an increase in ratio D/X (1, 2). As a result, there tends to occur an acceleration of inflation (3, 4, 5, 6,) which, given the relation implicit in curve SA, leads to a lower level of S/X (8) compared with the initial situation (0). From the standpoint of the dynamics of acceleration, the existence of curve SA guarantees that the above-mentioned movements will be sustained and lead to intensifying pressure toward acceleration. However, there is an additional element which corresponds to the shift in curve SA, since reductions in S/X mean shifts of the curve to the right, and these shifts increase the reductions in S/X.

Now let us examine the dynamic implications of the interactions between acceleration and the ratio $b \cdot j/c$. Figure 22 will illustrate these, assuming a vertical curve SA and a stable curve DS. A ratio of S/X below the critical level (0) would lead to an acceleration of inflation, as explained above (1, 2, 3, 4, 5, 6). This acceleration, as pointed out in the discussion of the determinants of the ratio j/c, tends be accompanied by an increment in this ratio. From the standpoint of the model, this would represent an increase in the angular coefficient of curve GD (7). The increase would be even greater if parameter b also increased with the acceleration of inflation, reflection a deterioration in the conditions for financing the public sector. This variation in the angular coefficient would cause an even sharper acceleration of inflation (15), even if ratios S/X and D/X (6, 8. . . 15) were assumed to be stable.

Thus, even if the total public debt per unit of output were kept constant through appropriate combinations of economic policy measures, inflation might not be stable. In an economy with the characteristics in question, any type of acceleration of inflation will cause persistent rises in the ratio $j \cdot b/c$, and these in turn tend to sustain the acceleration.[29]

Having seen the dynamic implications of each of the relationships implicit in curves SA, DS, and GD, we can now go to figures 23 and 24 to verify their interaction. Starting from a ratio of S/X below its critical level (0), figure 23 shows first of all that this leads to a larger total public debt per unit of output than the previously existing one (0, 1, 2). This increase both shifts curve DS downwards (3) and tends to increase the acceleration of inflation (2, 4, 5, 6, 7). The acceleration

Figure 21

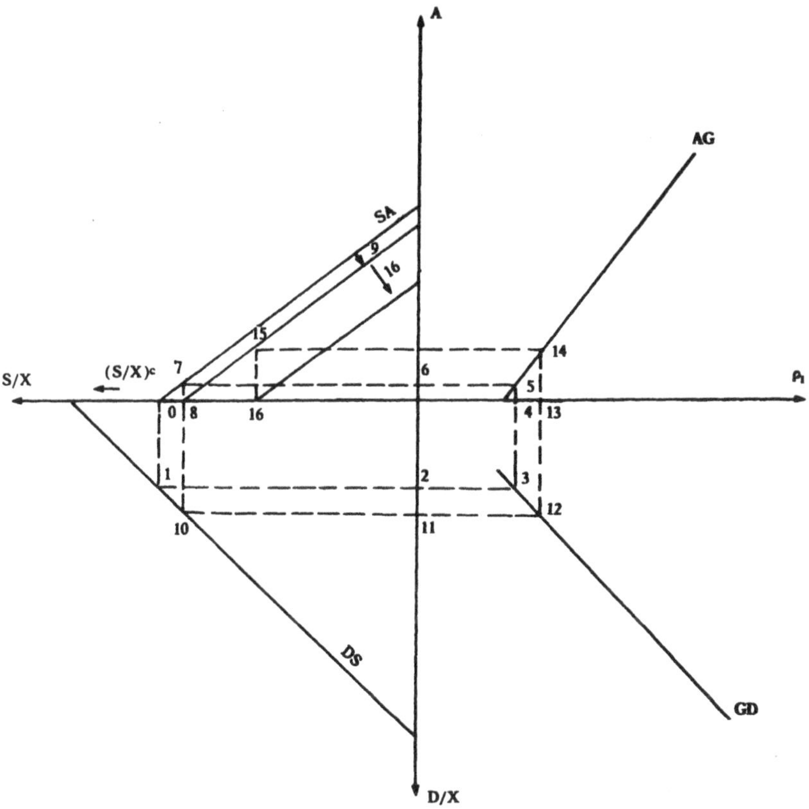

Figure 22

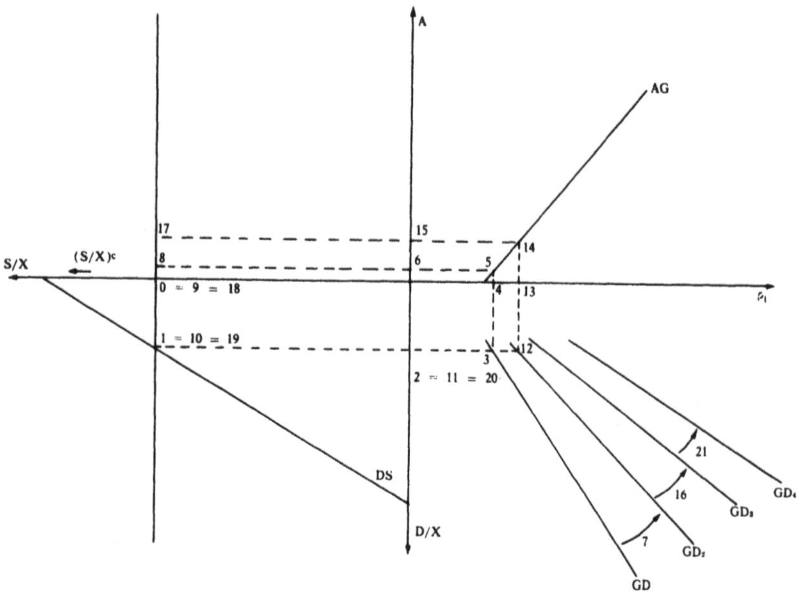
A
AG
17
15
14
S/X
(S/X)c
8
6
5
0 = 9 = 18
4
13
1 = 10 = 19
3
12
2 = 11 = 20
21
DS
16
GD4
GD3
D/X
7
GD2
GD

Figure 23

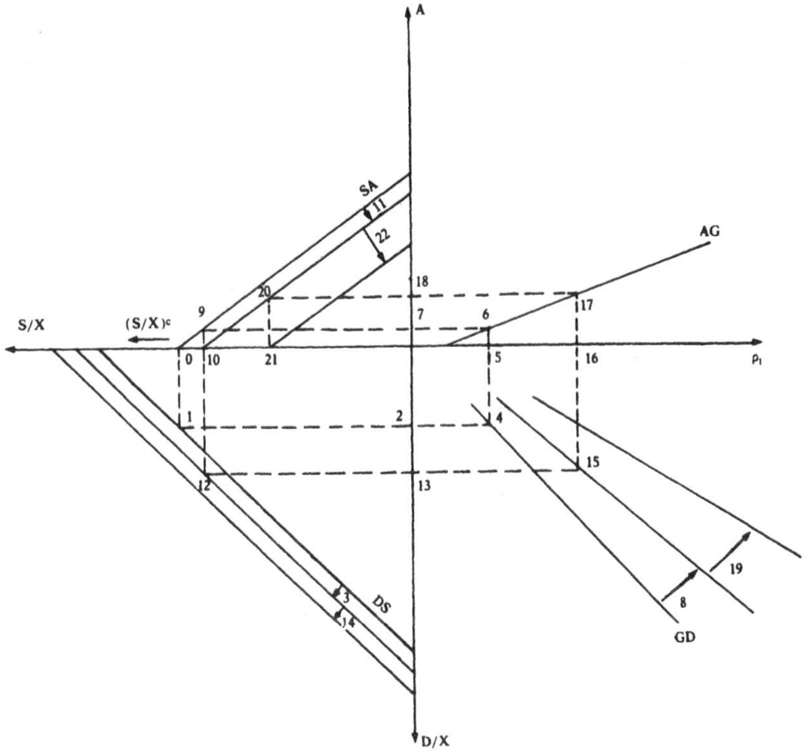
A
SA
11
22
AG
18
20
9
7
6
17
S/X
(S/X)c
0
10
21
5
16
P1
1
2
4
15
12
13
19
8
3
DS
14
GD
D/X

Figure 24

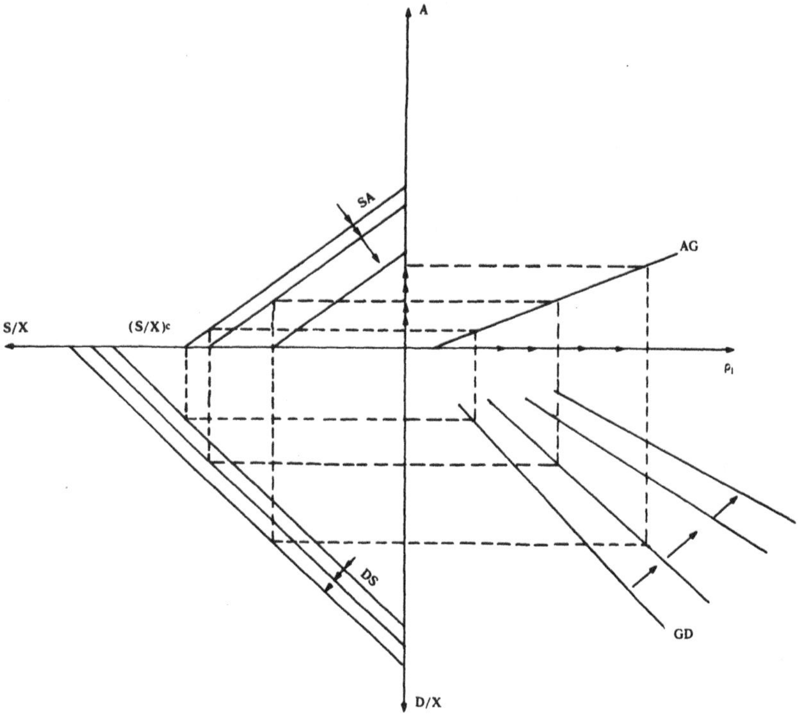

in turn tends to reduce the ratio of S/X (7, 9, 10), moving curve SA to the right (11), and tends to increase the ratio $b \cdot j/c$, thereby increasing the angular coefficient of curve GD (8). The reduction in the value of S/X associated with the shifts in S/X and $b \cdot j/c$ makes the tendency for inflation to accelerate even stronger, and this, combined with the shift in curve SA, will lead to a major drop in the ratio of S/X. This process tends to be progressive, as shown in figures 23 and 24, exacerbating the tendency for inflation to accelerate and causing progressive deterioration of public finances.

In sum, an adjustment process tends to incur strong public-sector indebtedness which, if it is not adequately accompanied by an increase in the public-sector operating surplus per unit of output,[30] eventually leads to a growing debt per unit of output. Given the adjustment situation and the impossibility of significantly reducing the ratio $b \cdot j/c$, increased public-sector indebtedness tends to lead to an acceleration of inflation, which is sustained both because of the progressive rise in D/X and because of the dynamic repercussions of the acceleration on $b \cdot j/c$ and S/X, directly, and on D/X, indirectly.

6.8 The Model Representing the Basic Interactions of the Acceleration of Inflation and Attempts to Contain Inflation

For obvious reasons, governments endeavor to neutralize, or at least take the sting out of the processes accelerating inflation through explicit or implicit economic policy measures.[31] These measures may be designed in an immediate way to combat acceleration or to control and/or restore to health the finances of the public sector.

As for the former type of measure, when based on real depreciation of public-sector prices and charges or on some explicit or implicit form of subsidy, their effects will be, at the start, to dull the acceleration of inflation and, after that, to cause an even sharper acceleration because of negative effects on the financial situation of the public sector.

In other words, when governments realize that inflation shows signs of accelerating, they may introduce a policy for damping down the acceleration by containing public prices

Figure 25

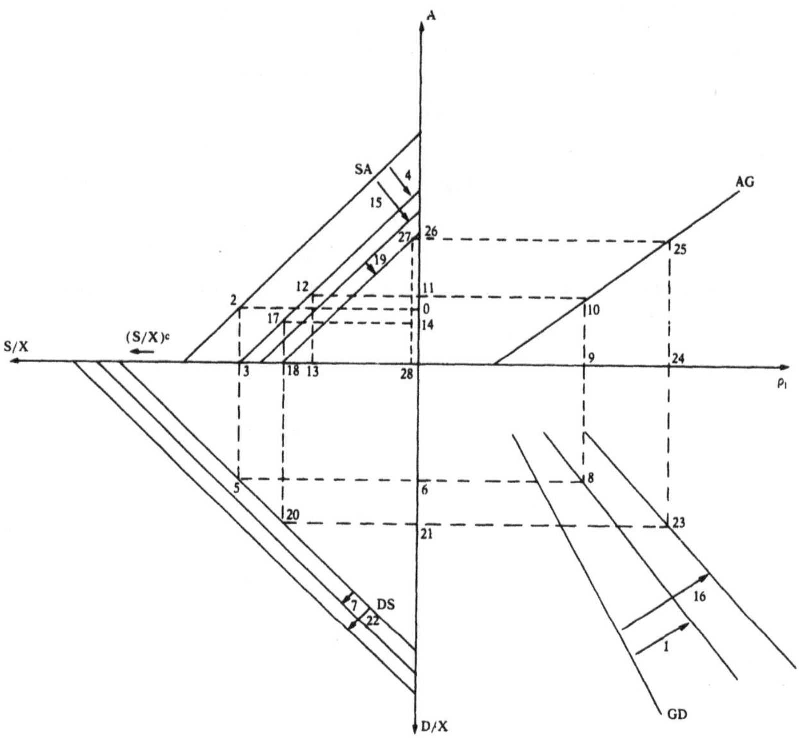

A
SA
4
15
AG
27
26
25
19
12
11
2
0
10
17
14
S/X
(S/X)c
3
18
13
28
9
24
p_1
5
8
6
20
23
21
16
7
DS
22
1
GD
D/X

and charges or by granting special subsidies. Although in the short term these measures can brake inflation, they eventually lead to a reduction in S/X and a rise in j/c, so that acceleration later bounces back with a vengeance. This can be seen by comparing circuits (0 . . . 13) and (14 . . . 28) in figure 25. The first circuit shows the dynamics of a situation identical to that presented in figure 23, which portrays a context where economic policy remains passive. The second circuit shows the dynamic results of a policy of containing acceleration of inflation through depreciation of public-sector revenues. As the figure shows, the second circuit starts from a lower level of acceleration (14) than that which corresponds to a passive economic policy (0).

However, this is achieved at the cost of a shift in curve SA (15) and an increase in the angular coefficient of GD (16). These changes lead to a larger debt per unit of output (21 instead of 6), whose effects are amplified by a larger ratio $b \cdot j/c$. As a result, although the process begins with a lower initial acceleration rate than the rate which would occur if economic policy remained passive, a situation finally arises where not only the acceleration rate (26) is higher than the rate corresponding to passive economic policy (11) but also the ratio S/X (28) is well below the ratio S/X which would result from the alternative of nonintervention by government (13). The government could attempt to reduce acceleration again by resorting once more to the expedient of containing its own revenues. But this practice, while capable of producing results in the short run, would lead to even greater inflationary pressure in the future.

Another type of policy, this time one with greater chances of success in the medium term is the reinforcement of the financial situation of the public sector.[32] This approach is highly dependent on special political conditions and on a not-too-high level of financial maladjustment. Let us examine the effects of two alternative policies of this kind: (a) a policy of relatively mild financial reinforcement of the public sector, i.e., one which is clearly insufficient to raise the ratio S/X enough to pass its critical value (policy type 1);[33] (b) a policy of strenuous reinforcement of public finances, whose

Figure 26

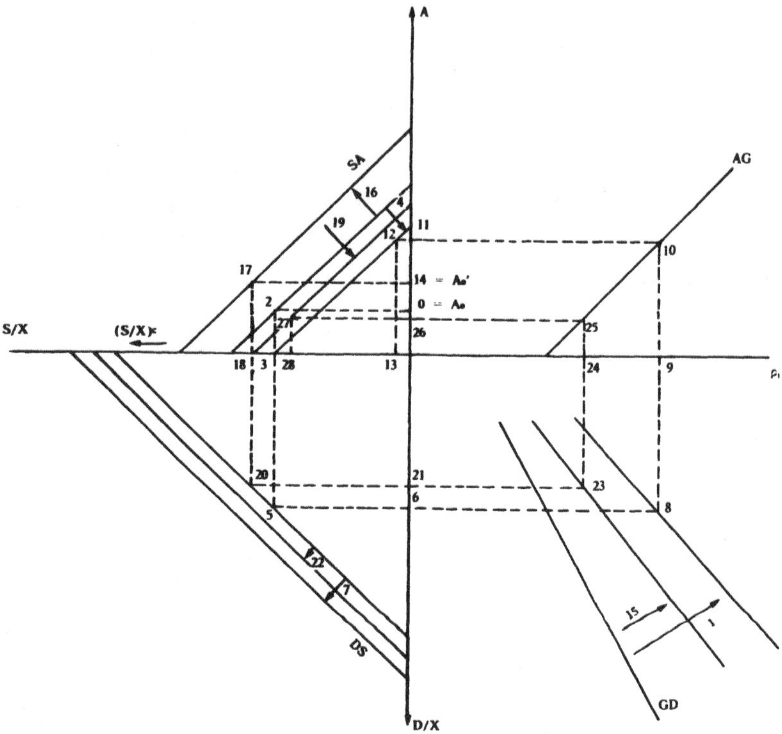
A
SA
AG
16
4
19
11
12
10
17
14 = A₀'
2
0 = A₀
S/X
(S/X)*
27
26
25
18
3
28
13
24
9
20
21
23
6
5
8
22
7
DS
15
1
GD
D/X

immediate effect would be to obtain a higher S/X than its critical value (policy type 2).

Figure 26 shows a comparison of the effects of policy type 1 with those of a passive economic policy. The circuit (0 . . . 13) corresponds to the latter situation, while circuit (14 . . . 28) shows the effects of policy type 1. This comparison demonstrates that such a policy, whether of mild or strenuous financial reinforcement, leads initially to a sharper acceleration of inflation than that which would occur if economic policy remained passive.

However, the increase in the ratio S/X (16) and the smaller increase in the ratio $b \cdot j/c$ (15), compared with the situation of a passive economic policy (1), would tend to push acceleration to a lower level (26) than that of the initial situation (14).[34] Moreover, in a manner diametrically opposed to a policy of fiscal concessions as a way of decelerating inflation in the short run, if policy type 1 were implemented the ratio S/X would tend to grow larger (28) than it would be if the government did not intervene (13).

Nevertheless, a policy of mild financial reinforcement, whose fundamental advantage would be to prevent secondary elements from giving the acceleration process a boost and making the results of such a policy unforeseeable, would end up with a lower S/X (28) than its critical level. Hence the acceleration would tend to maintain the trend resulting from the basic processes synthesized in figure 23.

As an alternative to policy type 1, a policy of strenuous financial reinforcement of the public sector could be implemented. To assist in analyzing its dynamic effects, this alternative will also be broken down into two parts: (a) a "miscalculated" policy of strenuous fiscal reinforcement (policy type 2a); and (b) a policy of fiscal reinforcement with chances of success (policy type 2b).

Figure 27 shows the results of policy type 2a. Circuit (0 . . . 16) is very similar to circuit (14 . . . 28) in figure 26, corresponding to policy type 1. The differences are as follows: the fiscal reinforcement, by definition, would lead initially to a larger S/X than its critical value (3) and would maintain it above that level in spite of the initial acceleration of inflation which this policy would bring about (1, 4, 5). Since this

Figure 27

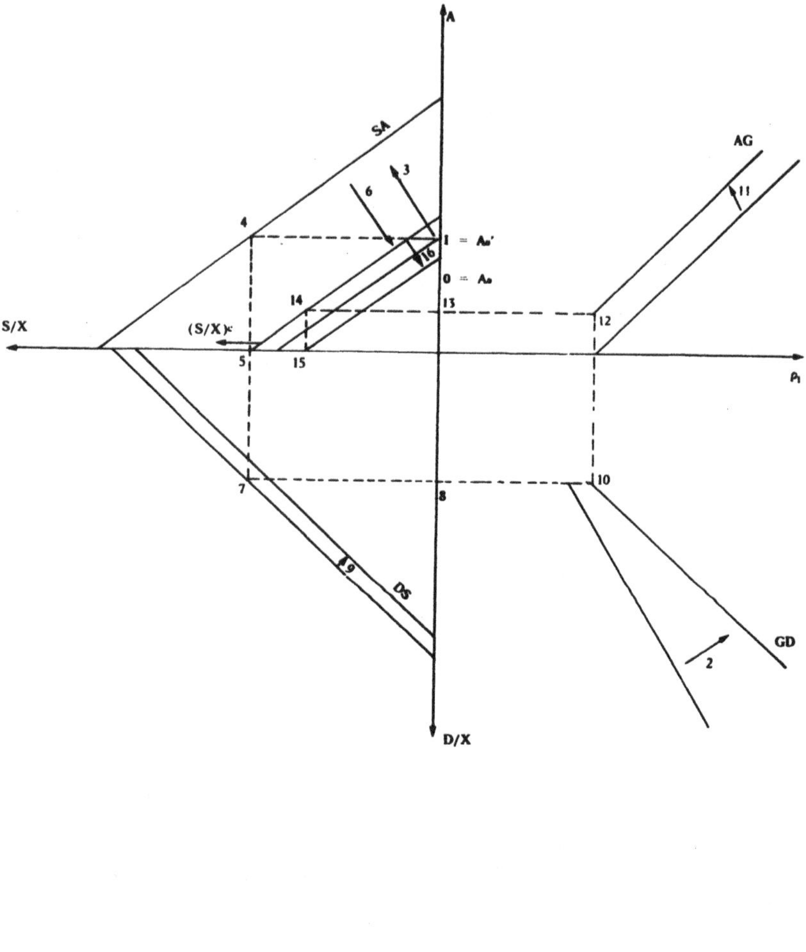

level of S/X following the initial acceleration of inflation (5) would still be higher than its critical level, ρ_t could possibly diminish, depending on the behavior of $b \cdot j/c$ and d.

However, given that the initial acceleration of inflation caused by the immediate effects of the shock would have been extremely strong, there would tend to be a reaction of the secondary elements, which would be translated as an increment in acceleration (11, 12, 13), regardless of the fact that ρ_t could be dropping or even reaching the value of 1. The resulting acceleration associated with S/X slightly higher than its critical value could lead to an additional reduction (13, 14, 15) in S/X, which would bring this ratio back below its critical value. From here on the dynamic shown in figure 23 would be reintroduced. Thus, figure 27 shows that implementation of a policy of financial reinforcement of the public sector, even if it were strong enough to produce an initial improvement in S/X compatible with stable inflation, has immediate inflationary effects associated with the reaction of secondary elements which could jeopardize the full effectiveness of such a policy. The problem stems from misforecasting the inflationary effects of a policy of strenuous fiscal reinforcement.[35]

Finally, let us consider the policy with chances of success. This is a situation where the dynamic effects in terms of acceleration and its consequences would lead to reductions in the value of S/X that do not lower S/X below its critical value. The expansion in the public-sector operating surplus would be large enough for later reductions in the surplus, caused both by the initial acceleration associated immediately with implementation of the fiscal measures and by the acceleration resulting from the action of secondary elements, to lead to a level of S/X which would still be higher than its critical level.[36]

Thus, in theory it would be wrong to discard the possibility of a fiscal adjustment that could improve the financial situation of the public sector. However, there are a number of problems in the designing and implementation of such a policy.

The outcome of this kind of policy may be decisively jeopardized by the strong "waves" of acceleration which tend to be formed. As pointed out above, these waves consist of (1) the immediate effects of implementing a policy of this type, i.e., the direct inflationary impacts of such a policy, and (2) the inflation "waves" resulting from chain reactions of the secondary elements triggered by the sharp acceleration caused by a policy of this type. Thus to achieve stabilization under the circumstances in question the adjustment has to be much greater than would seem necessary at first glance. The adjustment would be characterized by uncertainty regarding its results, given the impossibility of forecasting precisely how much inflation will accelerate owing to the effects produced by implementing the policy.

In theory it is possible to imagine a fiscal reinforcement which is capable of realizing three objectives:

(a) considerably increasing the value of S/X so as to stabilize ratio D/X;
(b) establishing a safety margin to avoid the problems of inflation waves caused by a policy of this type;
(c) building up sufficient reserves to guarantee neutralization of the effects of future inflation shocks likely to occur in the short run.

However, such a fiscal reinforcement would not be politically palatable, and would moreover be of doubtful effectiveness. It is worth examining why in more detail.

As stated above, it is theoretically possible that a policy of type 2 might be successful. There are some major problems, nonetheless. First, in an economy of the type discussed here, any acceleration of inflation would easily re-create a situation where S/X fell below its critical level. For this reason it would be necessary to set a certain safety margin when implementing policy type 2. The fiscal reinforcement required must be significant not only because of the high degree of current maladjustment in public finances characteristic of such economies, but because of two additional factors: the need for an extra preventive expansion of S/X to offset the losses that would tend to occur because of the dynamic effects of a policy of this type; and the need to create a safety margin against the effects of renewed inflationary shocks.

From the formal standpoint, therefore, the solution for an attempt to stabilize the inflation rate could be obtained through a system of equations representing the basic relations in the model. Specifically, the fiscal effort required for stabilization would have to be equal to the current maladjustment magnified by factors corresponding to the dynamic effects of acceleration on the financial situation of the public sector, to the expected reactions of secondary elements, and to expectations regarding the possibility of future inflationary shocks. Thus the theoretically possible solution reflects the need for a fiscal shock whose intensity is proportional to the size of these factors and the gravity of the initial financial maladjustment. However, there are two additional problems.

On the one hand, as already mentioned, the fiscal reinforcement in question would have to be a significant one and would evidently depend on special political conditions, given the redistribution of income and, possibly, the recession it could provoke. Furthermore, the strong inflationary shock caused by this reinforcement would tend to trigger a progressive movement of curtailments in intervals between price and wage adjustments. This movement could be interrupted only through the imposition of earnings cutbacks on specific sectors or through a policy of fiscal concessions which would in turn reintroduce acceleration in the future, as shown by figure 25.

On the other hand, nothing could guarantee that the reactions of other secondary elements would follow the parameters established in the system of equations. These elements would depend on the reactions of the various economic agents in terms of shorter intervals between adjustments to earnings and changes in their indexation methods and expectations. In other words, while it is possible mathematically to arrive at a solution for a set of stabilizing measures, it remains true, as Keynes was fond of recalling long ago, that "There's many a slip 'twixt the cup and the lip."

7

FINAL REMARKS

The breadth and complexity of the subjects discussed in this book and, above all, the attempt to deal with old issues and relations in an innovative way make the task of summing up the central arguments especially difficult. I have therefore opted instead for some concluding remarks designed to highlight a number of questions that may have been insufficiently stressed because of the method of exposition.

(1) Economists tend to agree that existing theoretical knowledge of inflationary processes is far from adequate. In my opinion the main reason is that economists themselves usually leave aside a crucial aspect of such processes: the fact that they are historically determined.

(2) With this in mind, I set out to obtain a theoretical grasp of acceleration of inflation in chronically inflationary economies with significantly productive structures and undergoing adjustment.

(3) The existing theoretical frameworks were not appropriate because they were based on microfoundations that did not suit the object of analysis. For this reason my first step was to construct an alternative theoretical framework to understand short-run variations in prices and desired markups on the basis of microfoundations that are not in flagrant contradiction with the nature of a capitalist economy. The key features are the idea that the economic structure is inherently unstable, and the adoption of an appropriate conception of the way in which expectations are formed and incorporated into the pricing process, returning to the idea of user cost developed originally by Keynes.

(4) Using this new theoretical framework, I endeavored to show that when a situation of public-sector financial fragility

is reached, the economies under consideration here develop an endogenous component of acceleration, and hence suffer from accelerating inflation.

(5) I developed a number of new concepts, such as public-sector financial fragility. This is not the same as the concept of public deficit. It is a combination of high total public indebtedness per unit of output and the bankruptcy or breakdown of the existing schemes for financing this debt. I tried to show that this is the relevant concept for an analysis of such acceleration, contrary to the approach adopted by conventional thinkers.

(6) The financial situation of the public sector is an important variable in determining inflation. However—and this point is fundamental—it is necessary to understand the mechanism by which the financial problems of the public sector are passed on to prices in a form which is compatible with microfoundations adequate to the study of capitalist economies. The usual argument is that prices are affected by the public deficit through monetary expansion or cost pressures created by increases in the interest rate. In this book I put forward an entirely different argument, in which the expectational dimension of prices plays a fundamental role—a role which becomes dominant in the process of acceleration in a situation of public-sector financial fragility. Utilizing the concepts of user cost and of public-sector financial fragility, and recognizing that economies have a structure—that is, are made up of many productive sectors with differing patterns of utilization of inputs—I show that because of its impact on the user-cost index of public-fiscal goods, the financial fragility of the public sector leads to acceleration as a result of pressure for changes in relative prices which arises among the sectors with differing patterns of utilization of public-fiscal goods. This acceleration eventually produces a number of dynamic effects which exacerbate the financial fragility of the public sector and the acceleration of inflation itself.

(7) When I refer to economies with accelerating inflation, I do not mean that economies in such a situation will necessarily present permanently rising inflation rates. The rise in inflation is a trend which can be attenuated or offset

by compensatory forces, such as income concentration and absorption by government of financial losses in favor of private groups. However, these compensatory forces tend to become progressively weaker as inflation accelerates, whereas the endogenous component of acceleration tends to become stronger as the financial fragility of the public sector increases.

NOTES

Chapter One

1. The economic literature does not contain an established concept of what a chronically inflationary economy is. In my own view, this is not something which can be established statistically. An economy is chronically inflationary, I would contend, when it presents a recurrence of inflation rates considered high and systematic enough to make the conclusion of economic contracts unviable without indexation clauses. In some countries, which I would term chronically inflationary, the costs of renegotiating contracts and collecting information are so great that the parties to a contract prefer to minimize them by including a clause providing for automatic adjustment in line with a general price index. On this subject, see Frenkel (1986).

2. "It has long been obvious that the roots of inflation—whether in Western Europe, the United States, Latin America, or elsewhere—lie deep in the social and political structure in general, and in social and political conflict and conflict management in particular. The disputes among Keynesians, monetarists and other economists about the causes of inflation deal with the modeling of inflationary processes that unfold among the various spheres and sectors of economic activity and, consequently, with the improvement of economic policymaking. But it would be difficult to find an economist who would not agree that underlying social and political forces play a decisive role in causing both inflation and the success or failure of anti-inflationary policies" (Hirschman 1985, 53).

3. I see adjustment processes (described in chapter 5) as deriving from the exhaustion of a scheme for financing the economy, externally and internally; they include both situations in which specific adjustment policies are applied and situations in which their application is only a possibility.

4. In chapter 5 I define what I mean by a significantly complex productive structure.

5. "On the other hand, it is sometimes possible to identify as causes of price acceleration circumstantial facts which could also give grounds for defining other types of inflation. For example, financial crises (due in part to real factors or to fragilities in banking systems) lead potentially to intense demand for inflation to reduce the real value of liabilities. The mechanism whereby inflation is generated may initially involve greater monetary expansion or increases in certain prices. Depending on where the emphasis is placed, these mechanisms may be focused on as may the specific origin of inflationary pressures" (Heymann 1986).

6. It would be wrong to omit the remark that this point of view is not the consensus either. For some authors, certain controversies result from the lack of understanding on the part of other analysts that specific differences originate in the development of the techniques of economic analysis. An example is the argument recently put forward by Lucas on his divergence from the ideas of Keynes: "While Keynes and the other founders of what we now call macroeconomics were obliged to rely on Marshallian ingenuity to tease some useful dynamics out of purely static theory, the modern theorist is much better equipped to state *exactly* the problem he wants to study and then to study it" (Lucas 1987, 2).

7. That is, monetarist, new classical and neostructuralist theories.

8. The chronically inflationary countries with a significantly complex productive structure and with economies undergoing adjustment.

9. This concept is discussed in chapters 5 and 6.

10. Goods which are produced and sold by the state, or highly subsidized goods, or again goods with a high real or potential tax burden attached to them.

11. Goods which are imported and/or intensively used in the production of exportable goods.

Chapter Two

1. It is precisely for this reason that the vast majority of economics textbooks deal with inflation under the heading of issues related to money and currency.

2. It is important to stress why the basic conception of economic structure is an important aspect of the microfoundations of inflation theories. It is well known that the question of the microfoundations of macroeconomics refers to the relations between theory expressed in terms of aggregates and the underlying behavior of the decision-making units (Dow 1985, 82). As will be shown

below, the basic conception of economic structure plays a decisive role in the coordination or lack of coordination of private behavior, which delimits the role prices can play and conditions the elasticity of expectations.

3. One might also mention a Mengerian type of price formation, which would correspond to strictly subjective price determination. But as recognized by one of the most renowned members of this school, this conception still requires further elaboration: "Part of the explanation probably has to be sought in the fact that this Austrian theory of price formation, conceived like other Austrian ideas in the bright morning light of the early 1930s, has remained a project to this day. Nothing ever came of it. We may surmise that when the project is resumed the problem mentioned will have to be faced" (Lachmann 1985, 131).

4. According to the Arrow-Debreu version, general equilibrium can be expressed through relations between markets in which goods are differentiated in accordance with quality, location, date of delivery, and contingency: "Thus, for example, 'black umbrellas delivered in London on St Swithun's day 1995 if it is raining' would be a different good from similar umbrellas delivered at the same time and place in the event that it is not raining. The term used to denote goods defined in this way is 'dated, contingent commodities', for their availability is contingent on certain events (as is, for example, a payment under an insurance contract)" (Backhouse 1985, 289–290).

5. There are two versions of this hypothesis on the formation of rational expectations. The weak version accepts that economic agents have differing models of the economy, while the strong version assumes that they all have the same, correct model of the economy.

6. The idea that individuals use available information in the best possible manner is currently accepted by almost all schools of economists, including the post-Keynesians. However, the rational expectations hypothesis greatly restricts the idea of rational behavior, hence stopping short of full acceptance. "But the nature of reasonable behavior is severely constrained if disappointment of expectations is limited to stochastic deviation. By definition, expectations must be correct, given available information, in the sense of being distributed normally around the 'correct' prediction. Expectations need not be correct in the sense that the outcome in the next period must be what was expected in the first period; as long as the available information is incomplete, any equilibrium will be only temporary. But within any one period of mechanical time,

individual actions based on rational expectations must produce an outcome in that period which accords with those expectations. In the long run, the only information which is not available must take the form of random shocks" (Dow 1985, 149).

7. Especially in periods of low instability.

8. "His [Keynes's] work on probability suggested that reason had to act on limited information, and thus on subjective assessments of probability. Indeed Keynes came round to the view that reason and emotion cannot necessarily be treated separately. This rejection of the rational/emotional duality is consistent with the perception that Keynes rejected a dualistic mode of thought. Within the more holistic view of human nature which Keynes adopted (stemming from his analysis of the consequences of information problems), Shackle's concept of human imagination and creativity has been an important influence on Post-Keynesian analysis of the individual. Human behavior is thus *conditioned* by the environment in which actions are taken. In particular, Keynes emphasized the problems of decision-making under conditions of uncertainty. Lacking the capacity in many instances to form predictions, even in probabilistic terms, individuals employ conventions which rely heavily on group behavior" (Dow 1985, 99–100).

9. Ranging from the impossibility of situations disequilibrium (e.g., the view of advocates of pure equilibrium theory) to their possibility, where re-equilibrium is a long-term prospect whose course is not obvious, that is, where situations of disequilibrium do not automatically generate the mechanisms for short-term re-equilibrium. On the subject of theories of disequilibrium, also known as neo-Keynesian, it should be stressed that although they criticize and reformulate key aspects of general equilibrium analysis (see Felderer and Homburg 1987), they in fact share the conception of the overall stability of economic structures which I define here. The difference between them and more orthodox approaches is limited to the mechanisms and speeds of adjustment of the system when the latter is subjected to a disequilibrium-producing shock: "In more technical terms, the distinction (between those who prefer equilibrium or disequilibrium analysis) is the difference, according to Leijonhufvud (1968), between those who believe that the price mechanism has an infinite adjustment speed and those who believe that this speed is gradual or slow, implying a faster quantitative mechanism than the price mechanism" (Meller 1986, 282).

On the differences and similarities between the Walrasian and neo-Keynesian approaches, it is worth quoting Benassy's argument: "Starting from this basic insight, the non-Walrasian school has constructed a number of microeconomic concepts that allow the rigorous formalization of the functioning of individual markets and of the whole economy when demand and supply do not balance, and the mixed price-quantity adjustments that result from such situations. . . . We should finally note that the non-Walrasian method is not 'anti-Walrasian'; on the contrary, it applies the methods that have been so successful in Walrasian theory under more general assumptions" (Benassy 1986, 2–3).

10. On this point, see Possas (1986, 304–305).

11. "This means that capitalist economies are structurally and permanently subject to changes of greater or lesser magnitude and speed in their level of activity—changes which may cause fluctuations and even spark off crises; from this viewpoint, then, a capitalist economy is inherently crisis-prone" (Possas 1986, 305).

12. Although not all these combinations are consistent.

Chapter Three

1. Led by Milton Friedman, the endeavor to establish a differentiated analytical framework culminated in the publication of two important articles by Friedman in 1970 and 1971 in which he set out to show that Keynes's ideas and the quantity theory of money could be seen as two particular cases for equilibrium in the monetary and goods markets, when formulated in an appropriate manner. As an alternative to both theories, Friedman proposed a "third way" in which neither output nor the general price level are assumed *a priori* as constant. Instead of these assumptions, he took as the parameter defining the system the nominal rate of interest, which in turn depends directly on the rate of growth of nominal income. For a presentation and analysis of Friedman's argument, see Chick (1973, chap. 7).

2. The political issue which runs through the entire debate between the leading schools of economics, labeled monetarist and Keynesian, centers on the role attributed to economic policy in running an economy. The main thrust of the monetarists was to try to show that the outcome of active policies (fiscal and monetary) is always negative—only the time it is said that the damage takes to be done varies according to the school of monetarism in question. Instead of activism, monetarists defend the establishment of permanent rules for economic policy.

3. For an analysis of the various versions of the Phillips curve, see Swaelen (1982).

4. On this point, see Swaelen (1982).

5. Objections will be made below to this argument, which, as will be seen, endogenizes the formation of nominal wages, which are exogenous in Keynes's original formulation.

6. Until Keynes, traditional economic thinking saw the labor market as a system of equilibrium in which real wages were the adjustment variable. Keynes, however, argued that real wages resulted from a more general, highly complex economic process, and that the workers negotiate pay in nominal terms.

7. The price rise which causes this error is explained as a consequence of an unexpected expansion in money supply, immediately translated into spending by units who see their portfolios as containing an undesirable amount of money, or into a drop in interest rates to below their natural level. This leads to a price rise, explained by the cumulative Wicksell effect.

8. The reason for the name "accelerationist version" has been neatly summed up by Santomero and Seater: "If raising the rate of inflation once and for all only lowers the unemployment rate temporarily, then the only way to keep the unemployment rate permanently below the natural rate is by continuously increasing the rate of inflation—i.e. by accelerating prices" (Santomero and Seater 1978, 516).

9. See Simonsen (1983, 279).

10. This does not mean that there are no important problems in this Friedmanian interpretation of the Phillips curve. For a synthesis of the problems and a presentation of an alternative neoclassical model, the Gray-Fisher model, see Simonsen (1983, 298–300 and 477–482). For more about the expectational argument of the Phillips curve, see Laidler (1981, 12–21).

11. What lies behind this idea is a view of overall equilibrium, where money is a good just like any other. Monetary expansion leads to a rise in demand for goods directly or indirectly through a fall in interest rates: "Similarly, if an added supply of money is dropped like rain upon the system, people will adjust. In part, they may raise their net supply of loans in the financial market, lowering the interest rate on securities (non-money). That in turn raises D, encouraging substitution of the good for money and thus raising the price of the good. In part, they may directly raise their demand for goods as a result of the added money, again raising the price of the good" (Okun 1981, 8).

12. On this point see Laidler (1981, 15–21).

13. This assumes a lack of elasticity in the system regarding creation of money, resulting from the hypothesis of the exogeneity

of money. A critique of this hypothesis is given at the end of the analysis of monetarism.

14. On this subject it is relevant to note that Tobin (1972) and Hicks (1974), in their theories of the labor market, endeavored to highlight the inadequacy of seeing labor-power as a commodity like any other: "Both theories share a fundamental axiom: In modern industrial society one cannot analyze the goods and the labor markets according to the same economic principle. In goods markets the contact between two parties ends the moment the transaction (a sale or purchase) is completed. In contrast, the demand for or the supply of labor implies that both market participants expect to have a lasting relationship, at least for a certain time, similar to that expressed in rental or lease contracts. Workers as well as firms have an interest in seeing that the labor contract is fulfilled in accordance with the agreed conditions, since changes give rise to adjustment costs for both sides (Poole 1976). According to Hicks, continuity is the principle that differentiates the labor market from the auction market for goods. The wage contract regulates the relationship between the two participants in the labor market for a certain period of time" (Frisch 1983, 160).

15. "In this market, it is a rational interest of the firm to establish a long-run relation with a certain group of workers. Part of the work at a firm is firm-specific: this firm-specific skill is either acquired by the worker himself in the so-called learning-by-doing process, or the firm allocates a certain amount for training of its workers, which they then further develop in the course of work. The firm tries to keep those workers who have proved efficient in the work assigned to them. Employers are generally interested in keeping their experienced workers, because the value they produce exceeds the value which the less experienced ones produce by more than the wage difference between the two groups of workers. Employers are uncertain about the capabilities of outside potential employees. They do know, however, who are the best, the more experienced workers among those already working at their firm. They wish to keep the wages of these workers above the nearest most advantageous possibilities offered in the labor market in order to reduce the number of their employees quitting. Therefore they do not reduce the wages even under unfavorable demand conditions, because if they did so they might lose those workers on whose employment they insist most; instead, while keeping the wage level unchanged, they dismiss those whose work is less profitable. They will retain the most efficient and the cleverest workers even if their labor is momentarily not needed, because they assume that sooner or later

the business cycle will turn in their favor. And when demand for a firm's products increases and it wishes to employ more workers, it need not increase the wage rate to recruit the necessary labor force, because as a result of the higher wages paid in the 'career' market, workers seeking jobs will queue up at the firm's gate even at the earlier wage rates, and thus it has an ample source of labor to draw from. The experienced workers will not quit even if their wages do not rise in the upsurge, because their skills are firm-specific, so that they would hardly be able to utilize them in another job and thus their wages would be lower elsewhere. But there are also a number of other advantages that tie them to the firm, such as the benefits of the seniority system, bonuses, old-age pension programs etc." (Mátyás 1985, 597–598).

16. On this point, see also Piore (1979).

17. For Friedman, wealth is any asset which can generate income. Thus, for example, a wage is a form of income derived from human capital.

18. On this point, see Seligman (1962).

19. Friedman's "obstinacy" in refusing to recognize the specific nature of money can be understood from the perspective of his Walrasian view of the economic structure, in which money cannot be thought of as a store of value: "Keynes's central critique (1936) is that the Walrasian model of general equilibrium does not use the concept of money as a store of value. In the Walrasian-neo-classical world, with competitive markets, perfect information about the future and a Walrasian auctioneer to guarantee instant simultaneous equilibrium throughout the period t, it becomes totally irrational to hoard money as a store of value while there are other financial assets which provide positive profitability" (Meller 1986, 293–294; my translation). On the relation between uncertainty and money, see Davidson (1972, chap. 6).

20. According to this approach, individuals demand money only for transactions. Demand for money M^d could be represented by a constant proportion of real income (Y) multiplied by the general price level (P). This constant proportion, known as the Cambridge constant (k), establishes the relation between demand for money and money income as follows: $M^d = k \cdot PY$

21. This is precisely one of the points which characterize post-Keynesian economics as a body of theory standing apart from the major group of theories known as mainstream macroeconomics.

22. "Endogeneity refers to the capacity for institutions to create new money instruments, or for new financial institutions to emerge,

to satisfy excess demand for money. It is certainly widely recognized that attempts by monetary authorities to control the supply of money by one definition tend to be thwarted by such institutional responses" (Dow 1985, 188).

23. The basis for new paradigms has been laid since this movement began. The most relevant trends are the New Classical school, the pure theory of equilibrium, disequilibrium theory, post-Keynesian theory and the neo-Austrian school.

24. On this point see the work of Sargent and Wallace (1975).

25. For an example of a macroeconomic model which is representative of inflation analysis according to the new classical approach, see Frisch (1983, 131–37).

26. "The rationally expected rate of inflation is therefore the difference between the systematic component of the rate of growth of the money supply $E(mt/I(t-1))$ and the trend rate of real economic growth x^*. An increase in the expected rate of expansion of the money supply leads immediately to an increase in the expected rate of inflation" (Frisch 1983, 134–35).

27. See my remarks in chapter 2 on the unstable nature of capitalist economies.

28. See also the introductory remarks on the various models of expectation formation discussed in chapter 2.

29. See Taylor (1983, chap. 11).

30. For a description of the key characteristics of this school, see Taylor (1983, chap. 1). For a presentation of the main differences between this school and structuralism, see Heymann (1986).

31. According to the neostructuralists, mechanisms of adjustment in an economy tend to lead it to a long-term dynamic equilibrium determined by two basic relations, external equilibrium and internal equilibrium. I return to this point later on.

32. On the concept and dynamics of flexprices and fixprices, see Hicks (1974).

33. The inverse of average labor productivity.

34. For details see Taylor (1983, chap. 2).

35. See Sunkel (1958). The essence of structuralist thinking is summed up as follows by Lopes: "This theory explains inflation as the outcome of the structural transformation which accompanies economic development. Industrialization and the population shift from the country to the towns put pressure on a relatively rigid supply of agricultural products, forcing a change in relative prices in favor of agriculture which is reflected in a generalized increase in prices. The rigidity in the supply of agricultural goods

is explained as deriving from the structure of ownership in agriculture and from the impossibility of obtaining agricultural goods from abroad because of the economy's limited importing capacity. This balance-of-payments constraint in meeting the demand for imports generated by industrialization also accounts for additional inflationary pressure, through exchange-rate devaluation or a drop in the supply of previously imported goods. In all cases, however, the essence of the phenomenon is a structural transformation which requires a change in relative prices, and in the presence of a certain inflexibility for some prices to move downwards such a change can occur only via inflation. It is obvious that if the required inflation is not permitted by a passive policy, the consequence will be a fall in the rate of economic growth" (Lopes 1979, 10–11, my translation).

36. For details of the way in which these expressions are derived, see Taylor (1983, chap. 2).

37. Strictly speaking there are various ways of defining inertia. I return to this point below. On the relation between development of the inertial tendency hypothesis and studies of wage dynamics, Lopes remarks: "This inertia hypothesis regarding inflationary tendencies was suggested to me by the Brazilian experience with pay policy" (Lopes, 1985).

38. On the conceptual distinction between shock and inflationary tendency, see Lopes (1985).

39. As I have remarked earlier, explanations of the inertial component vary from the argument elaborated by Frenkel as summed up above to other arguments which I refer to below.

40. These two relations of equilibrium form the basis on which all neostructuralist models are built. They take on various forms, both in terms of detail and in terms of the pairing of variables which comply with the conditions for equilibrium. However, as I have already pointed out, they always maintain that open economies must satisfy the same equilibrium relationships.

41. For the detailed deduction of these curves and their macroeconomic parameters, see Bacha (1982, chaps. 4–6).

42. According to this conception economic policy plays the role in the short run of speeding up the process of adjustment to point E, a point of equilibrium, in figure 8. In the medium run, it modifies the macroeconomic parameters so as to enable the macroeconomic equilibrium to become established according to a more favorable rate of growth in potential output and rate of inflation.

43. Bacha explains the reasons for the gentler slope of SK on p. 180 of the work quoted.

44. For a broader discussion of the macroeconomic parameters which define the internal and external equilibria, see Taylor (1983) especially on the monetary and financial aspects (chaps. 5 and 6).

45. In the case of Brazil, according to Arida (1984), given the peculiarities of the financial system, in which passbook savings deposits are indexed to past inflation but yield a fixed rate of annual interest, elasticity significantly different from 1 in terms of the expected monetary expansion as compared with past inflation would not be consistent with any prospect of financial stability. On the concept of expectation elasticity, see Hicks (1946).

46. On the same article, Simonsen attempts to show formally how inertia results from a rational process of decision making in a non-cooperative game with *n* persons and imperfect information. Also using game theory, Cortázar argues that the explanation of the inertial tendency does not require an imperfect information hypothesis: "The assurance game of price determination that takes place under competition and a 'passive' monetary policy is yet another explanation of the persistence of inertial inflation. And one does not require the assumption of imperfect information that characterizes other interpretations" (Cortázar 1987, 16).

47. On the problems created by orthodox stabilization policies there is a vast literature, of which the outstanding examples are Taylor (1983), Foxley (1983), Dornbusch (1982), and Díaz-Alejandro (1981).

48. The difference between the structuralist and neostructuralist treatments of external shocks must be seen in the differing contexts of the debate with conventional schools. In the discussion with monetarists in the 1950s and 1960s, structuralism sought to highlight shocks as endogenous to the overall development process. With the acceleration of inflationary processes in the 1970s, and the increasing importance of propagation mechanisms, the main weapon for fighting the monetarist approach became emphasis on the inertial component. In the context of this "new" discussion, the concern (of the neostructuralists by now) has been to concentrate on short-run phenomena, in which shocks take an exogenous form.

49. Since the early 1970s, capitalism has presented acute instability in the behavior of financial markets and of commodity and foreign exchange markets. See Tavares and Belluzzo (1986).

50. According to expression (17), the profit rate depends on the expected level of capacity utilization and on the markup. Thus assuming a fixed markup means presupposing the expectation that the level of capacity utilization will be relatively stable.

51. On this point see Davidson (1972, chaps. 3 and 6), and Tavares and Belluzzo (1986).

52. "Prices stop being 'normal' because calculation of long-run production prices now involves the cost of money (opportunity cost) and the user cost of strategic raw materials (particularly minerals), both entirely 'abnormal' costs. They are abnormal not just because interest rates or oil prices are high but because they fluctuate unexpectedly and sharply in the short run, and their long-run user cost tends to be altered abruptly and arbitrarily" (Tavares and Belluzzo 1986).

53. If the acceleration of inflation is exactly as predicted, the firm's actions will in no way boost the acceleration caused by the initial shock. However, if there is overestimation as a result of self-defensive measures, there will be an increment in the acceleration of inflation.

Chapter Four

1. For a critique of the traditional view of the role of prices and a proposition regarding their role in a capitalist economy, see Minsky (1986, chap. 7).

2. Desired markup must be distinguished from realized markup. Whereas the former is a function of the decisions made by individual capitalists and partially but directly determines the dynamics of inflation, the latter is a resultant variable depending on a set of decisions and their interactions, and which only indirectly acts as an influence on the dynamics of inflation through its influence on the process by which subsequent desired markups are decided.

3. Not all prices are determined directly by oligopolies. However, in an economy with a significantly complex productive structure, the weight and role of oligopolies in the production matrix, particularly in the case of manufacturers of producer goods, tend decisively to affect the evolution of all other prices, even though differences in velocity may be observed in the short run.

4. On this point see also Wood (1975).

5. This is a topic at the leading edge of industrial organization and has been a focus for specialists in this area of interdisciplinary work. On the principal structural determinants of markups and their significance, see Possas (1985).

6. For a critical summary of many of these contributions, see Possas (1985).

7. Marris 1963; Marris and Wood 1971; Baumol 1967; Wood 1975; J. Williamson 1966.

8. Simon 1955; Cyert and March 1963; Monsen and Downs 1965; O. Williamson 1964. The work of the parallel British group includes Andrews and Brunner 1975; Wilson and Andrews 1951; Downie 1958; Wiles 1956; Penrose 1959; Loasbey 1976.

9. Means 1962; Kaplan et al. 1958; Clark 1961.

10. Kalecki 1954; Sraffa 1960; Steindl 1952; Robinson 1962; Sylos-Labini 1962, 1974; Vickers 1968; Eichner 1973, 1976; Pasinetti 1981; Marris 1964; Coutts, Godley and Nordhaus 1978.

11. Eichner uses the idea of a "corporate economy", the essence of which is summarized on pages 29 to 35.

12. Cf. Henderson, 1954; Almarin Phillips, 1960. See also Almarin Phillips, 1961, 1962.

13. Eichner refers here to investments which cannot be funded with profit margins at their current level.

14. For a definition of this item and an explanation of its determinants, see Eichner (1976, 67 and 71).

15. For a definition, explanation and calculation, see Eichner (1976, 71–77).

16. ". . . These include (a) nationalization, (b) price regulation, (c) taxation, (d) tariff reduction, (e) release of government stockpiles, (f) qualitative restrictions of all types and antitrust prosecution."

17. "These three types of costs incurred by the megacorp, should it decide to increase the size of the average markup, can be converted into the equivalent of an implicit interest rate, R, by first applying the appropriate discount formulas" (Eichner 1976, chap. 3) "and then comparing the subsequent decline in cash flow, the latter being the equivalent of an externally borrowed principal sum for each year there is a net gain" (Eichner 1985, 38). A mathematical expression for the value of R is given in Eichner (1976, 302).

18. Strictly speaking, Eichner's original formulation deals with margins over average production costs and not margins over direct costs. It is my contention that the adaptation made here does not distort the grounds of his basic argument, however.

19. This unacceptable probability, i.e., the risk which the firm refuses to run, is associated not only with the objective loss of market share to the entering firm but, above all, with the risk of damaging its market hegemony, a decisive aspect of its operations: "Besides the very concrete loss of sales which the entry of a new firm can be expected to cause, there is a less tangible effect. The very ability to coordinate pricing decisions among the various members of the industry may be jeopardized by the intrusion of a new enterprise, one without a vested interest in price stability if it is to obtain some minimum share of the market. However, once a new firm has

been encouraged to attempt entry into an industry, it is not readily dislodged—even if the barriers it faces should turn out to be greater than anticipated. Whatever the returns, the new enterprise is likely to remain in the industry for some time, displacing the sales of the established firms and/or making price coordination more difficult. For these reasons, the prevention of new entry into the industry may have come to be viewed as essential to the optimization of a firm's long-run position" (Eichner 1985). In a confidence crisis, this limit may be lower still.

20. In economies undergoing adjustment these probabilities change significantly: the likelihood that new firms will enter diminishes considerably and the room to maneuver open to economic policy is seriously reduced by the external restriction both in terms of imports and the threat of a reduction in customs barriers, and in terms of the policymakers' ability to control and intervene.

21. On this point see Eichner (1976, 84).

22. In his 1976 formulation Eichner had established a horizontal curve, which in the 1985 version appears as a possibility depending on the conditions prevailing in the credit and stock markets, the conditions of the firm and the amount of funding required.

23. On the reasonableness of this assumption, see below, chapter 5.

24. "If technological change were not entirely capital embodied, the possibility would arise of being able to increase net revenue, and hence the total corporate levy realized in the long run, through investment in the development of cost-reducing methods. Similarly, if the megacorp-price leader were not committed to remain a member of but a single industry, the possibility would arise of investment in diversification. These possibilities, excluded from consideration here in the simple model, are nonetheless discussed in the later chapters" (Eichner 1976).

25. For Keynes, "capital equipment" is not confined to capital goods: ". . . a capital equipment, which term includes both his stocks of unfinished goods or working capital and his stocks of finished goods" (p. 52).

26. For an analysis of the basic determinants of pricing and production in Keynes, see Davidson (1972 chap. 3).

27. There are also involuntary capital losses, which in turn can be divided into losses associated with unavoidable but expected events, defined by Keynes as supplementary cost, and losses due to unforeseen processes, which he calls windfall losses: ". . . let us call the depreciation of the equipment, which is involuntary but not unexpected, i.e., the excess of the expected depreciation over the

user cost, the *supplementary cost*. . ." and further on: "There remains the change in the value of the equipment, due to unforeseen changes in market values, exceptional obsolescence or destruction by catastrophe, which is both involuntary and—in a broad sense—unforeseen. The actual loss under this head, which we disregard even in reckoning net income and charge to capital account, may be called the *windfall loss*." (pp. 56–57).

28. These latter two costs are also defined in an expectational manner, and can vary over time.

29. Keynes makes this point especially clear in the following passage: "In the case of raw materials the necessity of allowing for user cost is obvious;—if a ton of copper is used up today it cannot be used tomorrow, and the value which the copper would have for the purposes of tomorrow must clearly be reckoned as a part of the marginal cost" (Keynes 1965, 73).

30. This refutes analyses which see inflation only as a process resulting from the struggle to distribute an *income flow*. Recognition of the expectational dimension of pricing imposes the need to recognize that inflation must be understood as being *also* determined by a dispute among *stocks of wealth* in which not all economic agents can take part. It is basically a game among capitalists.

31. In the case of raw materials, determination of p_t is trivial. However, in the case of capital goods

$$p_t = \sum_{i=0}^{m-1} {}^t q_i / (1 - r_t')^i,$$

where ${}^t q_i$ is the yield expected in the period $t + 1$ and r_t' is the average interest rate expected in the period during which the yields referring to a capital good available in t would occur. Determination of p_0 in this case would follow the same procedure.

32. This includes interest payments on debts and dividends (see Eichner 1976), as well as an insurance payment. This replaces a risk cost inserted here by some authors, including Keynes, in relation to involuntary and unforeseeable capital losses.

33. As we will see shortly, t is an alternative way of representing the strategic determination of desired markups.

34. Here I closely follow Davidson (1972, 34), except for the part referring to "normal profit" which I have transformed into a separate unit because of my interest in highlighting its distinctive nature due to the strategic importance of desired markups under oligopoly.

35. Eichner argues that the executive group sees shareholders as a particular type of creditor (Eichner 1976).

36. This transformation is made to simplify the algebra presented in what follows.

37. Note that it is necessary for $h \cdot k < v \geq 1$ if p is to be positive. Since $h = j + d^* + s$, and k, d^* are given, this condition indicates that for s to be positive, the level of capacity utilization must exceed $k \cdot (j + d^*)$.

38. And $(1 - f)$ is raw material costs as a proportion of c.

39. This is an indicator of the intensity of utilization of fixed capital compared with other types of capital.

40. As well as permitting determination of the short-run variations of desired markups, this expression also makes it possible to recognize the determinants of the structural differences between desired markups in one industry and another.

Chapter Five

1. As this chapter develops I explain why adjustment processes constitute a situation of high instability, thus making the utilization of a constant markup unviable.

2. As stressed previously, I am fundamentally concerned with understanding the sustained acceleration of inflation, rather than the episodic external price and wage shocks that are usually the object of study.

3. See chapter 1.

4. A detailed analysis of these characteristics is contained in chapter 6.

5. Many of the statements made in what follows are general enough to be useful in the construction of an analytical framework for a study of inflation in countries which do not match the whole list of conditions given. However, the complete set of relationships and propositions set out here is designed to apply specifically to these economies.

6. For a detailed characterization of "corporate economy," its constituent parts, microfoundations, and the general features of its macrodynamics, see Eichner (1985).

7. On what I understand by chronically inflationary economies, see chapter 1, note 1.

8. The focus here is on countries undergoing adjustment. In such conditions the growing fragility of the public sector's financial position leads to a growing user cost of public-fiscal goods. In other words, the need for adjustment "transmits" the financial fragility of

the public sector to prices. This is why a growing debt-to-GNP ratio in the United States, for example, does not have the same effect on prices. The financial strength of the U.S. makes it possible to resolve the financial problems caused by a growing debt-to-product ratio by means of greater indebtedness. An economy under adjustment, on the contrary, is characterized precisely by the impossibility of easily increasing indebtedness. Even if this were possible, it would be seen by economic agents as a more and more unstable situation in the short term.

9. This aggravation has led some countries to such a serious state of financial fragility that it has ended up turning into an endogenous component of acceleration of inflation. Chapter 6 contains a demonstration of the endogenization of this acceleration under these circumstances.

10. Later I define what I mean by direct and indirect impacts of adjustment processes on inflation.

11. Until at least 1982 many countries increased their indebtedness even though conditions were highly precarious. From then on, the need to adjust—already pressing in several cases—became unavoidable.

12. This indebtedness was determined by: (a) internally defined needs for financing in each country; (b) external shocks in the terms of trade and interest rates; and (c) permissive practices by the banks resulting from price war and the struggle to hold on to and conquer market segments which marked the breakdown in the relatively stable oligopolized structure of the international private banking market which had prevailed up until the end of the 1960s. On this latter issue, see Devlin (1986).

13. On the impacts of interest rates as financial costs, see Lance Taylor (1983).

14. See chapter 1, note 10, for a definition of this term.

15. From now on I refer to such products as exchange goods.

16. Strictly speaking it is also possible to work with three similar categories for capital goods. However, this would merely introduce an unnecessary degree of sophistication into the formalization of my central argument, as will be seen below.

17. I refer not to any structure, but to a "significantly complex structure," as defined in the beginning of this chapter.

18. Canavese (1982) presents a reduced and common form of the structuralist models of inflation (for Latin America and for Europe) showing that pressure for changes in relative prices, wherever it may come from, can have differing results depending on the specification established in the model for the method of indexing to past

inflation the prices of the sector whose relative price is being pushed down. If indexing is partial, inflation will level off after it has risen. With full indexation, inflation will accelerate as long as there is pressure for changes in relative prices, and it will rise in proportion to the intensity of the pressure.

Chapter Six

1. In the large body of work on the impacts of adjustment policies, Foxley (1983) is outstanding.

2. As we saw in chapter 3, this component develops in such economies because of the generalized system for indexing wages to past inflation. This occurs as an outcome of the high cost of conflict and of obtaining information which an environment of systematically high inflation rates tends to create. The generalized indexation system acts as a basis for firms to adopt self-defensive behavior, but since they take decisions in an uncoordinated manner they end up using past inflation as a minimum reference point for adjusting their prices.

3. This fails to occur only when the government implements price and income controls or a freeze, or when a deceleration is caused by a chance event which by definition can have only a very short-term effect. In cases where prices and incomes are controlled or frozen, r tends toward a value close to zero. The more successful the policy for moving from the no freeze–no controls stage into the initial phase of the freeze or controls, the closer to zero r will be.

4. In this model, monetary policy does not play a key role in determining the course of inflation. My assumption is that in the context of chronic inflation, monetary policy tends to be immobilized for two reasons. First, monetary expansion cannot remain far behind the increase in price levels, since if it did so there would be a risk of a serious liquidity crisis. Secondly, given the enormous instability of expectations intrinsic to chronic inflation, if monetary expansion greatly exceeded the pace of price increases this could lead to an excessive reduction in interest rates. This reduction in turn would tend to raise the user cost of inputs and hence desired profit margins and prices, thereby causing a sharp acceleration of inflation.

5. By secondary elements I mean all the accelerating movements whose dynamics depend essentially, albeit not entirely, on the acceleration of inflation itself. These include the curtailment of the interval between adjustments of earnings for inflation; increases in self-funding margins (m^*) resulting from the increase in external

costs or reduced probability of the entry of new competitors; declining productivity; and other factors that come into play along with the acceleration of inflation (for an analysis of the various secondary elements in potential, see the equations on desired markups and prices at the end of chapter 5). These secondary elements catalyze the acceleration process, while also—under some circumstances—actually giving it a new boost by reintroducing acceleration. As I show below, this may occur when the financial situation of the public sector is very close to fragility. In this case an acceleration of inflation caused by a typically exogenous shock or by the action of a secondary element may trigger off the basic interactions of this acceleration, which from then on are enough to sustain it. These, then, are passive and secondary determinations of acceleration insofar as they tend to manifest themselves, apart from episodic circumstances, in a context of inflation already undergoing acceleration. It is not a question of a simple propagation mechanism, for the inflation rate itself goes up. In the model presented here, following the neostructuralist models with the hypothesis of the inertial behavior of inflation, propagation mechanisms are limited to the inertial component. The reason for making such a separation between secondary elements and what could be called the basic model—which, as already stated, represents certain economic interactions at the roots of the process of acceleration in economies with the characteristics in question—is to highlight the fundamental determinants of acceleration while simultaneously demonstrating as simply as possible the determinants of the endogenization of this acceleration.

6. The symbol /& means that the function "acceleration of inflation" is conditioned by parameters that reflect each particular productive structure.

7. Although user cost is a specific determination of each agent, there are general aspects which are of fundamental importance for determining the user-cost index of public-fiscal goods.

8. On this point see section 5.4.

9. The exposition which follows is introductory in nature, and does not specify all interactions. A detailed explanation of these will be given later on when I present the model itself.

10. Below I present a definition of public-sector financial fragility which is very close to the one proposed by Dreizzen (1985). Although the idea is basically the same, there are two differences. The first, more important difference is that Dreizzen presents this relation as if it were a general index without considering the differing conditions for financing each economy. This would seem to be a mistake,

as the public sectors of two countries may have the same ratio of financial expenditure to net revenue while facing entirely different situations. As shown in chapter 5, what defines fragility is the perception that there is an unsustainable relation between financial expenditure and net revenue, thus signaling a rise in interest rates. The second difference is that I have included the operating profits of state-owned enterprises in the government's net revenue.

11. This may be the case in other economies, such as those of the U.S. or Italy, where there is a high ratio of debt to operating surplus and the problems mentioned do not occur.

12. This parameter fundamentally depends on three conditions: (a) the supply of financing from the private to the public sector; (b) the supply of credit from the external sector; and (c) the average period for redemption of public-sector debt. Economies under adjustment and with chronic inflation are characterized by a scarcity of external credit and short average periods for redemption of debt. These conditions establish a high value for parameter b, so that even a relatively low ratio of $(j \cdot D)/(c \cdot X)$ can be translated into user-cost indices of public-fiscal goods which are greater than 1. But in economies where the supply of internal and external credits to the public sector is high and/or the average period for redemption of public debt is long, even a high ratio of $(j \cdot D)/(c \cdot X)$ may be compatible with a user-cost index of public-fiscal goods equal to 1, the parameter b would be relatively small.

13. Unless b and/or D/X are very low, making $b \cdot (j/c) \cdot (D/X) < 1$, in which case ρ_l would be equal to 1.

14. These economies have frequently even presented operating deficits.

15. See note 3 in this chapter.

16. Generally speaking, studies of the evolution of public debt per unit of output are limited to this ratio, although they allow for restricted hypotheses regarding the behavior of the public-sector operating surplus and the inflation rate. See for example Lerda (1987), Rossi (1987) and Braga, Welch, and De André (1987).

17. "This is known as the Laffer effect, which can also be extended to other taxes. The Laffer curve results from a very simple line of reasoning; whether the rate at which a tax is levied is zero or 100, collections will total zero (in the latter case because the basis for the tax is annulled). There must therefore be a rate of levy between 0% and 100% which can maximize collections. If the effective rate is higher, the tax base diminishes more than proportionally."

18. Here I refer specifically to the domestic interest rate, which tends to fluctuate at a high level.

19. On this point, see Dreizzen (1985).

20. "As we have seen, high inflation usually corresponds to a high level of variability in the inflation rate, with strong fluctuations in relative prices. This has two effects. First, for the firm it becomes more risky to undertake long-term commitments because an unexpected drop in the level of inflation (or in its cost-price ratio) may mean the impossibility of meeting the financial obligations contracted upon in the past. Second, the organization which grants credit finds itself, in view of this variability in absolute and relative prices, in serious trouble as regards evaluating the risks that the debtor will default. Given an adverse attitude to risk by both firms and banks, this leads to a shortening of maturities with the aim of permitting renegotiation at shorter intervals of the terms stipulated in loan agreements. On the other hand, it is common knowledge that arbitration of maturities is an essential function of the banks; the financial system must be able to transform short-term deposits into long-term loans, thereby running what is known as a "liquidity risk". But frequent and large-scale fluctuations in interest rates also introduce a significant "rate risk" for financial institutions. Hence intermediaries will prefer to make short-term loans in order to avoid the need to immobilize assets for long periods at predetermined rates, and finance them with short-term funds which must be raised continuously on the market at unforeseeable rates. Given the fluctuation in the rates offered by banks and the general uncertainty about relative prices and yields, depositors in turn will show a marked preference for short-term transactions so that they can be sure of the greatest possible liquidity and avoid capital losses" (Dreizzen 1985, 47–48).

21. "But to this it must be added that such phenomena not only shorten maturities but also in themselves aggravate the instability of the conditions prevailing in the financial market, and with regard to which the system is most vulnerable. Thus, for example, with chronic inflation the system is more vulnerable to increases in interest rates (because of the predominance of speculative and Ponzi positions); but these fluctuations in rates are in turn more frequent because of the instability" (Dreizzen 1985, 49).

22. On the tendency of governments to intervene in situations of financial instability, see the analysis by Minsky (1985) on the role of central banks as lenders of last resort.

23. The ratios to be established refer to trends which materialize only when other variables come into play. The real movement of inflation will also depend on compensatory forces which may derive both from unexpected and extraordinarily strong deflationary

shocks and from movements of economic policy, and again from the imposition of income losses on entire sectors.

24. This argument is based on the main hypothesis presented in Aghevaeli and Khan (1977; 1978), which states that public revenues tend to adjust more slowly than expenditures when inflation accelerates. This hypothesis was first developed by Oliveira (1967) and Tanzi (1977; 1978). These authors argue that the existence of time lags between the moment when taxes are generated and the moment they are collected means that revenues tend to drop in real terms when inflation accelerates, and that this depreciation of revenues grows worse as the acceleration intensifies. Secondly, Aghevaeli and Khan argue that the public-spending policies of governments in developing countries usually attempt to maintain spending at the planned levels in real terms, even when inflation rates are rising. Heller (1980) criticizes their hypothesis, noting that the various components of public revenues and expenditures behave differently in terms of the speed with which they adjust to inflation. Thus the effects of acceleration on the public deficit may be differentiated because of the differing structures of public revenues and expenditures. It is difficult, therefore, to establish a generally valid proposition about the behavior of the public-sector operating deficit when inflation accelerates. Nevertheless, this need not prevent us from accepting one insight of these authors which they fail to explore, namely that in most cases public spending tends to become relatively rigid in real terms once it has been planned for. I would argue, in support of the Aghevaeli and Khan hypothesis, that public spending tends to be sustained in real terms because, once planned, such expenditures lead to the formation of vested interests that bring strong, effective political pressure to prevent such spending from being significantly reduced in real terms. The same does not occur with revenues, evidently, and moreover revenues cannot be adjusted so easily because of the institutional constraints that prevent the introduction of new taxes or new methods for calculating and collecting taxes in the short run.

25. As already shown, the curve SA synthesizes that whenever inflation accelerates, the value of S/X drops.

26. For clarity's sake and to aid in accompanying the argument with reference to the figures, the numbers placed in brackets from this point on show the points and movements related to each result and interaction mentioned in the text.

27. In addition to the sequence of events outlined above regarding the situation described in figure 20, there is an additional aggravating factor which has to do with the evolution of the critical level

of the ratio S/X. As expression 11 in section 6.5 indicates, this critical level fundamentally depends on the public-sector debt per unit of output and on inflation tax. The influence of the former is trivial. The influence of the latter depends on the behavior of M^{-1}/X^{-1} in a context of accelerating inflation. For chronically inflationary economies reductions in M^{-1}/X^{-1} tend to reduce appreciably the second term corresponding to the critical value of S/X, and may more than offset the acceleration of inflation. Hence in these economies changes in the critical S/X ratio tend to follow closely the behavior of the total public debt per unit of output. The critical S/X tends to increase when D/X is growing, making the stabilization effort more and more problematic. This observation also obtains for all other situations described by the other figures in this section.

28. "As the inflation rate nears the tolerance threshold, an increasing number of labor unions begin to demand wage hikes before their agreements have run out. The employers eventually grant the hikes. But these will give inflation a new push and lead to a new curtailment in the interval between adjustments. The interval will probably be reduced to six months, and then in succession to three months, one month, a week and a day. At first the adjustments will be based on the cost-of-living index; but since publication of this index lags one, two or more months behind inflation itself, it is soon replaced with some other method. The best known and most up-to-date of all the indicators used in Latin America is the exchange rate for some foreign currency, usually the U.S. dollar" (Felipe Pazos 1978, quoted in Dornbusch 1986).

29. This would fail to occur only if the ratio S/X were sufficiently large to permit the government to absorb the effects of an acceleration of inflation, thereby avoiding expectations of an increase in ρ_l. Otherwise, if S/X is close to its critical level, any increase in $b \cdot j/c$ tends to lead to an increase in ρ_l.

30. From the standpoint of the model presented here, this means a value of S/X that is higher than the critical value.

31. In referring to implicit measures, I have in mind the fact that failure to adjust some charge, for example, may represent a very short-term anti-inflation measure, even though it has not been the object of an explicit economic policy decision.

32. I am assuming that the changes in public assets that would be required to solve at one blow the financial troubles of the public sector would be hindered by the absence of economic agents willing to realize such massive investments in a situation of high instability and high uncertainty, as is characteristic of adjustment processes

in economies with the features in question. In addition, I have also assumed that it would be extremely difficult to introduce property taxation at the level required to solve the public sector's financial problems. This difficulty would result in part from the risks of a major flight of capital out of the country.

33. The notion of "mildness" here would also be associated with the fact that in the short term such measures would be unable to produce a situation in which the secondary elements would react.

34. As already stated, this argument assumes that the fiscal measures involved would be mild enough to fail to activate the mechanisms corresponding to secondary elements.

35. This statement does not imply that it would be entirely possible to calculate this kind of inflationary consequence.

36. If this were achieved, no more would be assured than stabilization of public-sector financial fragility and, as a result, neutralization of a major dynamic factor in acceleration. To achieve price stabilization as well, the fiscal reinforcement would have to go beyond this neutralization and establish a relationship between the government's financial liabilities and its net revenues so that economic agents saw it as a stable one, i.e., not dependent on additional fiscal efforts. This would be compatible with a user-cost index of public-fiscal goods equal to 1.

REFERENCES

Aghevaeli, Bijan, and Mohsin S. Kahn. 1977. "Inflationary Finance and the Dynamics of Inflation: Indonesia, 1951–72." *American Economic Review* 67 (3, June): 390–403. Nashville: American Economic Association.

_____1978. "Government Deficits and the Inflationary Process in Developing Countries." *IMF Staff Papers* 25 (3, Sept.): 383–416. Washington, D.C.

Andrews, P. W. S., and Elizabeth Brunner. 1975. *Studies in Pricing*. London: Macmillan.

Arida, Pérsio. 1984. "Economic Stabilization in Brazil." Discussion draft. Rio de Janeiro: PUC.

Bacha, Edmar L. 1982. *Análise Macroeconômica: Um Texto Intermediário*. Rio de Janeiro: IPES/INPES (Série PNPE, 6).

Backhouse, Roger. 1985. *A History of Modern Economic Analysis*. Oxford: Basil Blackwell.

Baltar, Paulo E. A. 1985. "Salários e Preços—Esboço de uma Abordagem Teórica." Doctoral thesis. Campinas: Universidade de Campinas.

Barbosa, Fernando de Holanda. 1983. *A Inflação Brasileira no Pós-Guerra—Monetarismo versus Estruturalismo*. Rio de Janeiro: IPES/INPES (Série PNPE, 8).

Baumol, William J. 1967. *Business Behavior, Value and Growth*. New York: Harcourt Brace and World.

Benassy, Jean-Pascal. 1986. *Macroeconomics: An Introduction to the Non-Walrasian Approach*. Orlando, Fla.: Academic Press.

Boughton, James M. 1977. "Does Monetarism Matter?" *Economics* (Apr.):21–23. Indiana University.

Braga, Carlos Alberto Primo, John H. Welch, and Paulo de Tarso de André. 1987. "O Desequilíbrio do Setor Público Brasileiro: Cenários Alternativos." *Revista de Economia Política* 7 (3, July–Sept.): 5–17. São Paulo.

Brunner, Karl. 1970. "The Monetarist 'Revolution' in Monetary Theory." *Weltwirtschafliches Archive* 105 (1): 1–30. Tubingen.

Cagan, P. 1956. "The Monetary Dynamics of Hyperinflation." In *Studies in the Quantity Theory of Money*, ed. M. Friedman. Chicago: University of Chicago Press.

Canavese, Alfredo, J. 1982. "The Structuralist Explanation in the Theory of Inflation." *World Development* 10 (7): 523–529. Oxford.

Chick, Victoria. 1973. *The Theory of Monetary Policy*. Greymills Publishing.

Clark, John. 1961. *Competition as a Dynamic Process*. Washington, D.C.: Brookings Institution.

Cobham, David. 1978. "The Politics of the Economics of Inflation." *Lloyds Bank Review* (128, Apr.): 19–32. London.

Congden, Timothy. 1978. *Monetarism—An Essay in Definition*. London: Centre for Policy Studies.

Cortázar, René. 1987. "Inflation in Latin America: Old Lessons and New Ideas." Mimeo. Notre Dame, Ind.: Helen Kellogg Institute.

Coutts, Kenneth, Wynne Godley, and William Nordhaus. 1978. *Pricing in the United Kingdom*. London: Cambridge University Press.

Cyert, Richard M., and J. G. March. 1963. *A Behavioral Theory of the Firm*. Englewood, N.J.: Prentice-Hall.

Davidson, Paul. 1972. *Money and the Real World*. London: Macmillan.

Devlin, Robert. 1986. "La Estructura y Comportamiento de la Banca Internacional en los Anõs Setenta y su Impacto en la Crisis de America Latina." *Estudios Cieplan* 19 (June): 5–55.

Diaz-Alejandro, C. 1981. "Southern Cone Stabilization Plans." In *Economic Stabilization in Developing Countries*, ed. W. Cline and S. Weintraub. Washington, D.C.: Brookings Institution.

Dornbusch, Rudiger. 1982. "Stabilization Policies in Developing Countries: What Have We Learned?" *World Development* (Sept.). Oxford.

———1986. "Como Deter a Hiperinflação: Lições da Experiência Inflacionária Alemã da Década de 20." *Pesquisa e Planejamento Econômico* 16 (1, Apr.): 61–86. Rio de Janeiro.

Dow, Sheila C. 1985. *Macroeconomic Thought: A Methodological Approach*. Oxford: Basil Blackwell.

Downie, Jack. 1958. *The Competitive Process*. London: Duckworth.

Dreizzen, Jacobo Julio. 1985. *O Conceito de Fragilidade Financeira num Contexto Inflacionário*. Rio de Janeiro: BNDES.

Eichner, Alfred S. 1973. "A Theory of Determination of the Mark-up Under Oligopoly." *Economic Journal* 83 (332, Dec.): 1184–1200. London.

———1976. *The Megacorp and Oligopoly: Micro-Foundations of Macro-Dynamics*. Cambridge: Cambridge University Press.

———1985. *Toward a New Economics: Essays in Post-Keynesian and Institutionalist Theory*. London: Macmillan.

Felderer, Bernhard, and Stefan Homburg. 1987. *Macroeconomics and New Macroeconomics*. Translated from the German, Berlin: Springer–Verlag.

Fischer, St. 1977. "Long-Term Contracts, Rational Expectations and the Optimal Money Supply Rule." *Journal of Political Economy* 85 (1, Feb.): 191-205. Chicago: University of Chicago Press.

Foxley, Alejandro. 1983. *Latin American Experiments in Neoconservative Economics*. Berkeley: University of California Press.

Frenkel, Roberto. 1979. "Decisiones de Precio en Alta Inflación." *Estudios Cedes* 2 (3). Buenos Aires.

———1986. "Salários e inflação na América Latina: Resultados de Pesquisas Recentes na Argentina, Brasil, Chile, Colombia e Costa Rica." *Pesquisa e Planejamento Econômico* 15 (1, Apr.): 21–60. Rio de Janerio: IPEA.

Friedman, Milton. 1956. "The Quantity Theory of Money–A Restatement." In *Studies in the Quantity Theory of Money*, ed. M. Friedman. Chicago: University of Chicago Press.

———1968. "The Role of Monetary Policy." *American Economic Review* 58 (2, March): 1–17. Nashville: American Economic Association.

Frisch, Helmut. 1983. *Theories of Inflation*. Cambridge: Cambridge University Press.

Heller, Peter S. 1980. "Impact of Inflation on Fiscal Policy in Developing Countries." *IMF Staff Papers* 27 (4, Dec.): 712–748. Washington, D.C.

Henderson, Alexander M. 1954. "The Theory of Duopoly." *Quarterly Journal of Economy* 68 (4, Nov.): 565–584. Cambridge, Mass.: Harvard University Press.

Heymann, Daniel. 1986. *Tres Ensayos sobre Inflación y Políticas de Estabilizacioń*. Santiago de Chile: CEPAL, Documento de Trabajo no. 18.

Hicks, John. 1946. *Value and Capital*. New York: Oxford University Press.

———1974. *The Crisis in Keynesian Economics*. New York: Basic Books.

Hirschman, Albert O. 1985. "Reflections on the Latin American Experience." in *The Politics of Inflation and Economic Stagnation*, ed. Leon N. Tindberg and Charles Maier. Washington, D.C.: Brookings Institution.

Johnson, Harry. 1972. *Inflation and the Monetarist Controversy*. Amsterdam: North–Holland Publishing.

Kaldor, Nicholas. 1970. "The New Monetarism." *Lloyds Bank Review* 97 (July): 1–18. London.

Kalecki, Michel. 1954. *Theory of Economic Dynamics*. New York: Reinhart.

Kaplan, A. D. H., Joel B. Dirlam, and Robert F. Lanzilotti. *Pricing in Big Business: A Case Approach*. Washington, D.C.: Brookings Institution.

Keynes, John Maynard. 1965. *The General Theory of Employment, Interest, and Money*. New York: Harcourt, Brace & World, Inc.

Klamer, Arjo. 1984. *Conversations with Economists*. Totowa, N.J.: Rowman & Allanheld Publishers.

Lachmann, Ludwig M. 1956. *Capital and Its Structure*. London: London School of Economics and Political Science.

——1985. *The Market and the Markets*. Oxford: Basil Blackwell.

Laidler, David E. W. 1981. "Monetarism: An Interpretation and an Assessment." *Economic Journal* 91 (361, March):1–28. U.K.: Cambridge University Press.

Leijonhufvud, A. 1968. *On Keynesian Economics and the Economics of Keynes*. London: Oxford University Press.

Lerda, Juan Carlos. 1987. "A Dinâmica da Dívida Pública: de Domar–Lesner a Tobin–Simonsen." *Pesquisa e Planejamento Econômico* 17 (2, Aug.): 343–368. Rio de Janeiro: IPEA.

Lipsey, R. G. 1960. "The Relationship between Unemployment and the Rate of Change of Money Wage Rates in the United Kingdom, 1862–1957: A Further Analysis." *Economica* 27 (105, Feb.): 1–31. London: London School of Economics.

Loasbey, Brian J. 1976. *Choice, Complexity and Ignorance*. London: Cambridge University Press.

Lopes, Francisco. 1979. "Teoria e Política da Inflação Brasileira: Uma Revisão Crítica da Literatura." In *Resenhas de Economia Brasileira*, ed. João Sayad. São Paulo: Saraiva (Série ANPEC).

——1985. "Inflação Inercial, Hiperinflação e Desinflação: Notas e Conjecturas." *Revista de Economia Política* 5 (2, Apr./June): 135–151. São Paulo: Brasiliense.

Lucas Jr., Robert E. 1987. *Models of Business Cycles*. New York: Basil Blackwell.

Marfan, Manuel. 1986. "La Política Fiscal Macroeconómica." In *Políticas Macroeconômicas*, ed. René Cortázar. Santiago de Chile: CIEPLAN.

Marris, Robin. 1963. "A Model of the Managerial Enterprise." *Quarterly Journal of Economy* 77 (2, May): 185–209. Cambridge, Mass.: Harvard University Press.

———1964. *The Economic Theory of Managerial Capitalism*. London: Macmillan.

Marris, Robin, and Adrian Wood, eds. 1971. *The Corporate Economy*. Cambridge, Mass.: Harvard University Press.

Matyas, Antal. 1985. *History of Non-Marxian Economics*. Hungary: Macmillan Education.

Mayer, Thomas. 1978. *The Structure of Monetarism*. New York: Norton.

Means, Gardiner C. 1962. *The Corporate Revolution in America*. New York: Crowell-Collier.

Meller, Patricio. 1986. "Keynesianismo y Monetarismo: Discrepancias Metodológicas." In *Políticas Macroeconómicas*, ed. René Cortázar. Santiago de Chile: CIEPLAN.

Minsky, Hyman P. 1985. "Money and the Lender of Last Resort." *Challenge: Journal of Economic Affairs* 28 (1, March-Apr.): 12–18. New York: M. E. Sharpe.

———1986. *Stabilizing an Unstable Economy*. New Haven, Conn.: Yale University Press.

Modigliani, Franco. 1977. "The Monetarist Controversy or Should We Forsake Stabilization Policies?" *American Economic Review* 67 (2, March): 1–19. Nashville: American Economic Association.

Monsen, R. J. Jr., and Anthony Downs. 1965. "A Theory of Large Managerial Firms." *Journal of Political Economy* 73 (3, June): 221–236. Chicago: University of Chicago Press.

Muth, John F. 1961. "Rational Expectations and the Theory of Price Movements." *Econometrica* 29 (3, July): 313–335. Amsterdam, North-Holland.

Myrdal, G. 1953. *The Political Element in the Development of Economic Theory*. London: Routledge and Kegan Paul.

Okun, Arthur. 1981. *Prices and Quantities: A Macroeconomic Analysis*. Washington, D.C.: Brookings Institution.

Oliveira, Julio. 1967. "Money, Prices and Fiscal Lags: A Note on the Dynamics of Inflation." *Banca Nazionale del Lavoro Quarterly Review* 88 (Sept.). Rome.

Pasinetti, Luigi L. 1981. *Structural Change and Economic Growth: A Theoretical Essay on the Dynamics of Wealth of Nations*. London: Cambridge University Press.

Pazos, Felipe. 1978. "Chronic Inflation in Latin America." *Special Studies in International Economics and Development*. Irvington.

Pearce, David W. 1983. *The Dictionary of Modern Economics*. Hong Kong: Macmillan Press.

Penrose, Edith I. 1959. *The Theory of the Growth of the Firm*. Oxford: Basil Blackwell.

Phelps, E. S., and J. B. Taylor. 1977. "Stabilizing Powers of Monetary Policy under Rational Expectations." *Journal of Political Economy* 85 (1, Feb.): 163–190. Chicago: University of Chicago Press.

Phillips, Allen W. 1958. "The Relation between Unemployment and the Rate of Change of Money Wage Rates in the United Kingdom, 1861–1957." *Econometrica* 22 (100, Nov.): 283–299. Amsterdam: North–Holland.

Phillips, Almarin. 1960. "A Theory of Interfirm Organization." *Quarterly Journal of Economics* 74 (4, Nov.): 602–613. Cambridge, Mass.: Harvard University Press.

———1961. "Policy Implications of the Theory of Interfirm Organization." *American Economic Review* 51 (2, Feb.): 245–254. Nashville: American Economic Organization.

———1962. *Market Structure, Organization and Performance: An Essay on Price Fixing and Combinations in Restraint of Trade.* Cambridge, Mass.: Harvard University Press.

Piore, M. 1979. *Unemployment and Inflation: Institutionalist and Structuralist Views*. New York: M. E. Sharpe.

Poole, William. 1976. "Rational Expectations in the Macro Model." *Brookings Papers on Economic Activity* 2: 463–505. Washington, D.C.: Brookings Institution.

Possas, Mario Luiz. 1985. *Estruturas de Mercado em Oligopólio*. São Paulo: HUCITEC.

———1986. "Para uma Releitura Téoricia da Teoria Geral." *Pesquisa e Planejamento Econômico* 16 (2): 295–308. Rio de Janeiro: IPEA.

Purvis, Douglas. 1980. "Monetarism: A Review." *Canadian Journal of Economics* 13 (1, Feb.): 96-122. Canada: Book Review.

Robison, Joan. 1962. "The Basic Theory of Normal Price." *Quarterly Journal of Economy* 76 (1, Feb.): 1–19. Cambridge, Mass.: Harvard University Press.

Rossi, José W. 1987. "A Divida Pública no Brasil e a Aritmética da Instabilidade." *Pesquisa e Planejamento Econômico* 17 (2, Aug.): 369–380. Rio de Janeiro: IPEA.

Santomero, Anthony M., and John J. Seater. 1978. "The Inflation Unemployment Trade-Off: A Critique of the Literature." *Journal of Economic Literature* 16 (2, June): 499–544. Nashville: American Economic Association.

Sargent, I. J. 1982. "The Ends of Four Big Inflations." In *Inflation: Causes and Effects*, ed. R. Hall. Washington, D.C.: University of Chicago Press.

Sargent, I. J., and N. Wallace. 1975. "Rational Expectation, the Optimal Money Supply Rule." *Journal of Political Economy* 83 (2, Apr.): 241–254. Chicago: University of Chicago Press.

Seligman, Ben B. 1962. *Main Currents in Modern Economics: Economic Thought Since 1870.* New York: Free Press.

Simon, Herbert A. 1955. "A Behavioral Model of Rational Choice." *Quarterly Journal of Economics* 64 (1, Feb.): 99–118. Cambridge, Mass.: Harvard University Press.

Simonsen, Mario Henrique. 1970. *Inflação Gradualismo Versus Tratamento de Choque.* Rio de Janeiro, ANPEC.

_____1983. *Dinâmica Macroeconômica.* São Paulo: McGraw-Hill.

_____1986. "Rational Expectations, Income Policies and Game Theory." *Anais do XIV Encontro Nacional de Economia,* Rio de Janeiro: ANPEC.

Straffa, Piero. 1960. *Production of Commodities by Means of Commodities.* London: Cambridge University Press.

Steindl, J. 1952. *Maturity and Stagnation in American Capitalism.* Oxford: Basil Blackwell.

Sunkel, Osvaldo. 1958. "La Inflación Chilena: Un Enfoque Heterodoxo." *El Trimestre Económico* 25 (4, Oct.-Dec.): 570–599. Mexico: Fondo de Cultura Económica.

Swaelen, Edward J. A. 1982. *Desemprego, Salários e Preços: Um Estudo Comparativo de Keynes e do Pensamento Macroeconômico da Década de 70.* Rio de Janeiro: BNDES.

Sylos-Labini, Paolo. 1962. *Oligopoly and Technical Progress.* Cambridge, Mass.: Harvard University Press.

_____1974. *Trade Unions, Inflation and Productivity.* Lexington, Mass.: Lexington Books.

Tanzi, Vito. 1977. "Inflation, Lags in Collection and the Real Value of Tax Revenue." *IMF Staff Papers* 24 (1, March): 154–167. Washington, D.C.

_____1978. "Inflation, Real Tax Revenue and the Case for Inflationary Finance: Theory with an Application to Argentina." *IMF Staff Papers* 25 (3, Sept.): 417–451.

Tavares, M. C., and L. G. de Belluzzo. "Uma Reflexão sobre a Natureza da Inflação Contemporânea." In *Inflação Inercial, Teorias sobre Inflação e o Plano Cruzado,* ed. José Márcio Rego. Rio de Janeiro: Paz e Terra.

Taylor, Lance. 1983. *Structuralist Macroeconomics: Applicable Models for the Third World.* New York: Basic Books.

Thurow, Lester C. 1983/1984. *Dangerous Currents.* New York: Random House, Inc.

Tobin, James. 1972. "Inflation and Unemployment." *American Economic Review* 62 (1, March): 1–18. Nashville: American Economic Association.

——1981. "Diagnosing Inflation: A Taxonomy." In *Development in an Inflationary World*, eds. M. J. Flanders and A. Razin. New York: Academic Press.

Vanderkamp, John. 1975. "Inflation: A Simple Friedman Theory with a Phillips Twist." *Journal of Monetary Economy* 1 (1, Jan.): 117–122. Glasgow: Bell and Bain (North-Holland).

Vickers, Douglas. 1968. *The Theory of the Firm, Production, Capital and Finance*. New York: McGraw-Hill.

Wiles, Peter J. 1956. *Prices, Cost and Output*. Oxford: Basil Blackwell.

Williamson, John. 1966. "Profit, Growth and Sales Maximization." *Economica* 33 (129, Feb.): 1–16. London: The London School of Economics and Political Science.

Williamson, Oliver E. 1964. *Economics of Discretionary Behavior*. Englewood Cliffs, N.J.: Prentice-Hall.

Wilson, I., and P. W. S. Andrews. 1951. *Oxford Studies in the Price Mechanism*. Oxford: Clarendon Press.

Wood, Adrian. 1975. *A Theory of Profits*. London: Cambridge University Press.

www.ingramcontent.com/pod-product-compliance
Lightning Source LLC
LaVergne TN
LVHW101502200926
848483LV00001B/205

* 9 7 8 0 2 6 8 0 0 8 6 7 3 *